Fleming Mant Sandwith

Egypt as a Winter Resort

Fleming Mant Sandwith

Egypt as a Winter Resort

ISBN/EAN: 9783337252304

Printed in Europe, USA, Canada, Australia, Japan

Cover: Foto ©Andreas Hilbeck / pixelio.de

More available books at **www.hansebooks.com**

EGYPT AS A WINTER RESORT

BY

F. M. SANDWITH, F.R.G.S.

FORMERLY VICE-DIRECTOR OF THE SANITARY DEPARTMENT OF EGYPT

LONDON
KEGAN PAUL, TRENCH & CO., 1, PATERNOSTER SQUARE
1889

PREFACE.

Though much has been written about Egypt of late years, nothing especially for the guidance of invalids has appeared in the form of a handbook since 1867. The climate remains as it was then, but many of the surroundings are changed and improved, so that patients need no longer fear absence of civilization or undue expense. I have tried to avoid writing a guide-book, and to supply only that information which cannot be found in them. Baedeker's Guide-book is the best for Cairo and the Delta, but unfortunately has not been extended to Upper Egypt. Murray's Handbook was last published in 1888, but does not contain too much recent information, and Messrs. Cook have provided for their clients a very useful elementary book. I have to express my best thanks to many kind friends in Egypt and in England who have supplied me with necessary information, and I shall be grateful to those readers who will tell me of any errors.

F. M. S.

Cairo,
    October, 1889.

WORKS CONSULTED.

Petrie, F., ' Pyramids and Temples of Gizeh." 1883.
Walker, Dr., "Egypt as a Health-Resort." 1873.
Burney Yeo, Dr., "Climate and Health-Resorts." 1885.
Patterson, Dr., "Egypt and the Nile." 1867.
Smith, Dr., "Dictionary of Greek and Roman Geography." 1854.
Barbey, M., "Herborisations au Levant." 1882.
Dawson, Sir J. W., "Egypt and Syria." 1885.
Hull, Professor, "Survey of Western Palestine," etc. 1886.
Pruner, Dr., "Topographie Medicale du Caire." 1847.
Vyse, G. W., "Egypt: Political and Financial." 1882.
Williams, Dr., "Influence of Climate in Consumption." 1877.
Gastinel, Professor, "Étude des eaux de Helouan." 1883.
Reil, Dr., "Springs of Helouan." 1874.
Madden, Dr. T. M., "Health-Resorts of Europe and Africa." 1876.

CONTENTS.

CHAPTER		PAGE
I.	INTRODUCTION	1
II.	SUEZ CANAL—PORT SAID—ISMAILIA—SUEZ	12
III.	CAIRO	17
IV.	CAIRO (continued)	43
V.	EXCURSIONS FROM CAIRO	72
VI.	SUBURBS OF CAIRO—HELOUAN-LES-BAINS—PYRAMIDS—MATARIYEH	84
VII.	VOYAGE UP THE NILE	106
VIII.	LUXOR—ASSOUAN	119
IX.	ALEXANDRIA—RAMLEH	134
	APPENDIX	145

EGYPT AS A WINTER RESORT.

CHAPTER I.

INTRODUCTION.

This handbook is a humble endeavour to answer the queries of some of my esteemed medical friends in England and in the United States, who tell me they are sometimes at a loss to know what manner of patients they ought and ought not to send to Egypt. But, apart from the actual needs of invalids and their professional advisers, there is a large class of visitors who either accompany delicate friends abroad, or flee from their own homes merely to escape cold weather and bask in the sunshine. It is obvious that a health-resort which provides a suitable climate for invalids and a sufficiency of interest and occupation for healthy individuals will become more and more popular. The national interest which England has taken in Egypt since 1882, the growing prosperity and civilization which have attended the efforts of her officials on the spot, and the improved facilities for travelling obtained by Messrs. Cook, have all tended to make Cairo and the Nile a very favourite winter resort. Some six thousand visitors come to Cairo during the winter months, and of these about twelve hundred proceed up the Nile in steamer or in dahabiyeh. To show that the climate deals fairly with these masses of visitors, it may be mentioned that the writer, in a medical experience of six winters, has lost only two patients who came to Egypt for their health. Both these were patients far advanced in consumption, who ought never to have left their homes, one an Australian, who reached Cairo at the beginning of 1888, and died there in February; the other, an American, who died in December, 1888, a few hours after reaching Cairo. This experience is not only a personal one, for the death register shows that there have been only nine deaths among British visitors in Cairo during the six years ending June, 1889. Of these nine, seven arrived here ill of incurable diseases; the eighth was thought to be robust, but died of uræmic poisoning during her first week in Cairo; and the ninth caught a chill while out sketching, and died of double pneumonia. But the writer's object is not to try and prove that Egypt is the best health-resort in the world, but to give reasonable information about its climate to those who have practically decided against the respective merits of sea and mountain air, and are in search of pure dry desert air where rain is almost unknown, and where fog, strong winds, and cold are never felt.

At the outset it must be remembered that where the air is extremely dry, there the difference is the greatest between the maximum and minimum temperatures, for the sun's heat reaches the earth without difficulty by day, and again by night it disappears into space. Patients, therefore, can bask in Egypt in the temperature of an English summer by daylight, but must be prepared for autumnal cold after sunset. The summer months in England under favourable circumstances are well suited to those of feeble constitution, who can surround themselves in their own homes with modern luxuries, with the comforts which none but the English thoroughly study, and with all the pleasures of friends and family. But when the autumn cold requires such a one to take active outdoor exercise, for which he is not sufficiently robust, and when the absence of sunshine induces a depression of spirits in addition to his physical delicacy, he begins, if he is wise, to think of deserting his home comforts and of seeking a more cheerful climate like many migratory birds, whom he would do well to imitate. Judged by the thermometer, we find that the mean annual temperature of London is 50° Fahr., and the same isothermal line passes through New York, though the climates of the two cities are from other reasons widely different. The Royal Observatory at Greenwich supplies us with a daily average temperature for the last fifty years, and by consulting this we find that on October 19 the average temperature falls below 50°, descending in January to 36°, and never regaining 50° again till May. Roughly speaking, those fleeing from cold must leave England not later than the middle of October, and should not return there till at least the end of May.

Let us consider as fairly as possible the advantages and disadvantages of Cairo and the Nile for those in search of health.

The *advantages* are: (1) A dry and exhilarating air which acts in itself as a tonic, and enables visitors to be out-of-doors in sunshine the whole day. (2) An almost complete absence of rain, and of fog, and of clouded leaden skies. (3) The absence of extreme cold, so that the invalid by closing his windows at sunset need never breathe air colder than 55° Fahr., even without any artificial heat. (4) The absence of strong winds at Cairo and Luxor, though invalids occasionally require special protection on the Nile. (5) The interest and relaxation of mind inspired in a country where the remains may be studied of the ancient Egyptians, Persians, Greeks, Romans, Arabs, and Turks. (6) The presence in a perfectly oriental city of most available European luxuries, and a large and hospitable English society. (7) The absence of moribund phthisical patients, who find Egypt too far from home. (8) The facilities for riding and driving, and for playing all outdoor games.

The natives have a proverb, "He who drinks the waters of the Nile invariably returns to Egypt;" and in many instances this has seemed to be true, for nearly all strangers develop in a few months a great fondness for Cairo, and are grieved to leave it; while it can be honestly stated that most invalids either improve in health while in Egypt, or manfully hold their ground during their sojourn there.

The *objections* to Egypt as a health-resort are: (1) Its distance of six days or more from England, and of at least three days from the south of Europe, so that a sea-voyage is unavoidable. (2) The expense which naturally attends such a journey, the cost of hotels and *pensions* in Cairo, and the extra cost of a journey up the Nile. (3) The mosquitoes, which welcome young women and children very irritatingly, until they get used to mosquito-nets. (4) A certain monotony at the dinner-table of butcher's meat, poultry, and game. (5) The insanitary condition of the picturesque old parts of Cairo.

The climate of Egypt is, then, suitable during the winter months for a great variety of chronic ailments, among which may be mentioned—convalescence from pneumonia, fevers, and all acute diseases; that common delicacy of English youth which may be called "threatened phthisis," all cases of early phthisis, and all *quiescent* cases of the late forms of the disease; chronic bronchitis and emphysema; bronchial, catarrhal, and spasmodic asthma; chronic catarrhal affections of the larynx and pharynx, including "clergyman's sore throat;" rheumatism, rheumatoid arthritis, and gout in its various forms; heart-disease, and all other complaints which prevent a patient from walking or other active exercise; anæmia and chlorosis; exhaustion of nervous system from too great excitement, worry, business, or study, and sleeplessness or hypochondria; neuralgia, hysteria and its accompanying dyspepsia; diseases of spinal cord, locomotor ataxy, etc.; chronic kidney-disease; and the very large class of people without organic disease, who shrivel up sadly in a cold climate, and expand joyously in a sunny atmo-

Introduction. 7

sphere where they are not perpetually reminded of their sensitiveness to cold and to "taking cold." This last group includes those invalided home from India for malaria and other causes.

Cases of all these ailments have passed satisfactorily under the writer's observation during the last six winters.

But the most important question to try and solve is what kind of patients ought *not* to be sent to Egypt.

My personal opinion is that all cases of very advanced or rapidly advancing phthisis of both lungs would be better at or near home, unless the patients themselves express a decided preference for ending their days in a distant land. The friends of such patients often need to be reminded that mere change of climate will not cure the disease, but that wherever the sick man goes, he will undoubtedly take his disease with him.

Again, patients with dropsy and all the troublesome sequelæ of heart-disease are surely unwise to give up all their home-comforts and surroundings, unless their minds are wholly set upon going to a certain spot, and it seems cruel to prevent their carrying out the wish of their heart; but even then it is almost necessary that they should be accompanied by a trained nurse. A hot climate is perhaps too exciting for men with a tendency to apoplexy; but the sun at Cairo is not powerful till April, and then a helmet is sufficient protection.

Former writers have said that phthisis with a tendency to hæmorrhage should not be sent to Egypt; but I see no reason why they should not winter in Egypt, provided they exchange the undue stimulation of Cairo "khamseens" in April for the sea-breezes of Ramleh.

Phthisical patients with a previous history of hæmoptysis do not usually suffer from hæmorrhage in Egypt, and, moreover, it is not a common symptom in the cases of phthisis which one sees among the negroes and other natives of the country.

Outfit and Clothing.—Let us take this opportunity of telling our countrymen, and especially our countrywomen, that it is no longer necessary to buy from the outfitter the travelling kit which is based on patterns at least forty years old. Dust-cloaks, helmets, blue veils, goggles, pugries, and field-glasses are not becoming, and are not needful for walking or driving in Cairo. Let the visitor bring such clothing as he wears in England in the summer and autumn, and he will want little else beside. Flannel belts to be worn next to the skin are of great assistance in preventing attacks of diarrhœa. Helmets for wearing up the Nile can

Introduction. 9

be bought in Cairo. Pugries may be twisted around them, but it is of no use to wear streaming tails of coloured calico to protect the neck. If a helmet is objected to—and indeed few ladies look well in it—a Terai hat is the best substitute; but straw hats may be worn during the colder months. Flannel suits are always comfortable, and brown leather boots and shoes are commended to both sexes. Wire gauze goggles should be bought in England to protect delicate eyes from the glare of the sun and from sandstorms. Ladies who desire to ride must bring their habits, and will be more independent if they bring a saddle. Warm cloaks and rugs are wanted in December and January, and on the river always at night. Keating's powder or Persian powder is wanted for insects. Patent English or foreign medicines should be brought by the invalid if required, though the local druggists provide the public with the most commonly asked-for specialities. White umbrellas and all common requisites can be bought in Cairo.

Ladies may be glad of the hint that silk or silk and wool combination garments are preferable to underlinen.

Routes to Egypt.—Those who are not afraid of the sea can leave London by P. and O. steamers, or British India or Orient Line, and they will reach Ismailia in twelve days by paying £20.

Robust people who are not dependent upon the presence of a doctor and stewardess can economize by travelling from Liverpool to Alexandria by the Moss or Papayanni lines. For those who are not martyrs to sea-sickness, and to the general discomfort of life on board ship, there is no doubt that the sea-voyage is very healthy, very restful, and useful in gradually accustoming patients to change of climate.

Visitors who desire as little of the sea as possible must make their way to Brindisi, and then on to Alexandria by P. and O. or Austrian Lloyd; or from Trieste to Alexandria by Austrian Lloyd; or from Genoa or Naples by Rubattino to Alexandria; or from Marseilles to Alexandria by the Messageries steamers.

The passage from Brindisi to Alexandria takes three days and a half, and the whole journey from London to Cairo can be done any week in less than six days, at about the same expense as the long sea routes. Generally, it may be said, an English-speaking invalid is more comfortable on an English steamer, and it must be remembered that the large vessels which go on to India, China, and Australia, are often more luxurious than the smaller steamers which run only between Europe and Egypt. On the other hand, invalids must be warned that it is easier for them to land at

Introduction. 11

Alexandria than at Ismailia, because they may be obliged to traverse the Suez Canal by night, and then be put ashore uncomfortably in a boat in the early morning. Moreover, two trains run from Alexandria to Cairo in three and three-quarter hours, while from Ismailia to Cairo there is only one passenger train in the day, occupying four and three-quarter hours. At neither port is there any custom-house difficulty for personal baggage, and no passport is necessary.

Proposed itinerary.—Delicate patients should leave Europe at the middle or end of October, so as to arrive in Cairo early in November. Some remain in Cairo all the winter; others go up the Nile to Luxor in December or January, and return to Cairo at the end of February. In April they should go to Ramleh, and thence perhaps to Italy and the south of France, arranging not to reach England or other cold climates till the very end of May.

CHAPTER II.

SUEZ CANAL.

Port Said.

The visitor is not recommended to stay in any of the three towns on the Suez Canal, but he must pass through one of them unless he arrives from Europe by way of Alexandria. Port Said, with a population of about 10,500 natives and 6000 Europeans, is an impromptu insanitary town which originated in 1859 with the huts of the Canal workmen. It stands on a narrow strip of sand two hundred to three hundred yards wide, between Lake Meuzaleh and the sea, its site having been formed by dredgings from the harbour thrown into the shallow lake. The surface of the town is perfectly flat, and only about four feet above the sea-level, and the sandy soil is permeated by uncemented cesspools and underground reservoirs used by some of the inhabitants. It is dependent on Cairo for a water-supply *viâ* Ismailia.

It ought, of course, to be connected with Cairo by the railway, but this is strenuously objected to by those interested in the welfare of Alexandria. Visitors must either go half through the Canal and disembark at Ismailia, or alight from their steamer at Port Said into a small postal boat, which will carry them and their luggage to Ismailia in time to catch the train for Cairo. Port Said has a very small English colony, but possesses two English doctors, one in charge of the native hospital, the other living at the English hospital founded by Lady Strangford. The three hotels are not first class, but the traveller must often be dependent on one of them in making the journey from Cairo to the Holy Land. Meteorological observations are made at Port Said, Ismailia, and Suez by the Canal Company for transmission to Paris, but, as none of the towns can be considered a health-resort, it is unnecessary to quote them here.

Ismailia.

There is no prettier spot in Egypt than this little wayside town of 3500 inhabitants, most of whom are French and natives, and connected with the Canal Company and its works. There are two hotels, sometimes quite empty, and at other times, during the winter season, crowded to overflowing with hungry tourists. There are no places of interest to visit, and little to do besides sea-bathing in Lake Timsah, and donkey-riding along famous broad roads lined with sweet-smelling trees.

A fresh-water canal runs from Cairo to supply the waterworks, and the consequent mixture of fresh and salt water since 1869 is thought by the inhabitants to be responsible for the malarial fever for which Ismailia has of late years become unpleasantly noted in a country where malarial diseases are very rare.

There is a French hospital beautifully situated outside the town, and a French and a Greek doctor. The monuments now in the square at Ismailia, cut in Syene granite and diorite from Assouan, were brought from the ruins of Pithom, about twelve miles west of Ismailia. Pithom was apparently one of the garrison towns built by the Israelites for Rameses II. in the land of Goshen, and near it they encamped upon the second night of the Exodus, just as Lord Wolseley did in 1882 in the same district, now called Kassassin. The third night the fleeing Israelites halted close to Ismailia, and on the fifth day of their flight they are believed to have crossed the sea about halfway between Ismailia and Suez.

Ismailia is one of the cleanest and dullest towns

Suez Canal. 15

in Egypt, and was one of the healthiest until the boon of fresh water in great quantities after 1876 proved a curse by causing small swamps of water, which percolated through the desert sand from the new canals. The water-tanks in the gardens which used to supply the houses, and occasionally overflow, have been exchanged for a system of pipes and taps. Eucalyptus trees also have been planted, with a decided diminution of malaria.

Suez.

Suez is a town of 11,000 people, rather more English than either Port Said or Ismailia, and is of course the port of entry from India, Australia, and the far East. There is a comfortable hotel, an English doctor, and a railway line to Ismailia and Cairo, and a fresh-water canal supplying it from the Nile. Excursions may be made to the oasis called Moses' Well, to Ataka mountain, to the sea-coast to collect shells, or to Suakin.

Suez is in the same latitude as Cairo, and the Ataka range stretches across the desert to join Mokattam there.

Naturalists tell us that at Suez begins a genuine tropical sea, differing entirely in its inhabitants from the Mediterranean, only one day's journey north of it. Hermit crabs and very many others of the crab family, bivalves and univalves, star-shaped egg-urchins (*Echinometra lucunter*), crustaceans, sponges, and coral-fish, with many scores of others, can be found by exploring the coast and rocky pools.

By means of a boat on a clear day, a visit to the coral reefs may be made, though the best coral is at some distance from Suez. Dark brown and yellowish green coral in loose and brittle bits is based here on massive rocks of black mesh coral (*Porites*), and more rarely there may be found the cherry-red cup-star variety (*Pocillopora*)—not to be confounded with the ordinary red coral, which is not found here.

The strange and wonderful fishes can be best seen by going to the market, no less than five hundred and twenty kinds which haunt the coral slopes being known. One often offered for sale is the ball-fish (*Tetredon*), which has the power of blowing itself up like a balloon and floating on the water on its back; this, like the urchin-fish (*Diodon*), is protected like a hedgehog on land by spiny prickles, beside a beak something like a parrot's. They can bite well with their beaks, but are not poisonous. Small sharks are occasionally heard of, leaping and flying-fish, and the gay parrot and rainbow fishes are also known.

CHAPTER III.

Cairo.

The capital of Egypt and seat of government is six days by post from London, $2^{h\cdot}$ $5^{m\cdot}$ $9^{s\cdot}$ east of Greenwich, and in north latitude 30° 4′ 40″.

Geology.—Every one knows that the Delta is an alluvial plain, literally the gift of the Nile, and that Cairo, succeeding to old Memphis, is at the apex of the Delta. The Mokattam hill of limestone rises about six hundred feet (above sea-level) behind the present town, and, as its fossils and nummulites show (*Echinolampas Crameri*, etc.), its age is that of the Eocene Tertiary, and its sides were washed by the Mediterranean waters in the days before the Delta was formed into a shallow bay with a sandy bottom. Near Mokattam is the Red Hill, 320 feet above the sea, of Miocene or Oligocene period, with sinter conglomerate containing silicified trees, probably deposited within the area of an inland lake. At Mokattam, towards the Red Hill, are purple and yellow sand and fine gravel, with a little marl and clay and fragments of *Terebratula, Ostrea, Pecten,* and *Balanus,* all considerably later than the Eocene period, and tending to show that there was once another sea margin 220 feet above the Mediterranean and Red Sea. Near the Pyramids again are raised beaches, limestone pierced by *Pholades* and *Ostrea undulata;* and two miles south of the Sphinx are fossil sea-urchins (*Clypeaster Egyptiacus*), oyster-shells and pectens (? Post-Pliocene). The geological map shows alluvial deposit everywhere in the Delta and along the banks of the Nile, while to both east and west of this near Cairo is nummulite limestone, and to the north-east of Cairo are sandhills in the desert stretching down to the Suez Canal. The incomparably dry pure air of Cairo and Upper Egypt is due to this same nummulite limestone desert, which for miles and miles acts as a great lung of nature and purifies all the air which blows across it, while the extraordinary fertility of Lower Egypt is caused by the alluvial deposit. The absence of vegetation and of moisture in the desert has left its characters almost unaltered for ages, though there is abundant evidence of mountain torrents in prehistoric times and in the present day.

Lower Egypt consists geologically, therefore, of— (1) Nummulite limestone of the Eocene period, stretching southwards in the desert from Cairo and Suez, on the east of the Nile valley, and again on its west beyond the Pyramids; (2) a little calcareous sandstone (Miocene) containing trunks of petrified trees; (3) raised beaches of a more recent time, made of gravel, sand, and seashells, near Cairo and Suez; (4) alluvial deposits forming the Nile valley and Delta; and (5) recent sandhills marking the old centre of the bay of Lower Egypt, in the days when the Mediterranean washed the Mokattam heights and the terrace on which the Pyramids now stand.

Near Cairo there are in the desert numerous dry river-beds, telling of the time when there was an abundant rainfall, and the wild elephant, which has now retreated south of the Soudan, could take his fill of water and green food. The existence of ravines and rounded pebbles must not be taken as evidence of a great rainfall in prehistoric times, for even to-day, although there is so little rain in Cairo, there are sometimes in the hills above Cairo very heavy torrential storms, which, although the quantity of rain is not great, sweep down the valleys and actually cover the neighbouring fields with a yellow mud and with small pebbles.

Enough has been written to show that the alluvial soil deposited by the Nile is an entirely foreign element in the geological formation of Egypt, and it may be easily studied in the perpendicular sepia-coloured mud-banks, which vary slightly in colour, and have occasional thin layers of drifted sand intervening. Wherever there is no alluvium, which is of course the only soil in Egypt, there is sterile desert, and this is the charm of Luxor, and of the suburbs of Cairo. The Nile soil is stated to be unlike any other in the world in composition.

The Royal Society, with the aid of the Royal Engineer Corps stationed at Cairo, has made several borings through this soil to the old floor of the Delta. The mixtures of blown sand and Nile alluvium were found to continue down to the depth of 121 ft. from the surface, and 95 ft. below the level of the Mediterranean. At that depth a remarkable change in the deposits took place, and beds of gravel containing both pebbles and subangular fragments of quartzite, chert, compact limestone, with some metamorphic and igneous rocks, were found, and similar beds occurred at intervals down to the greatest depth reached. Up to the present time no contemporaneous organic remains have been found in these deposits. The borings near the Nile at Cairo in 1883 may be briefly summarized thus: For 6 ft. beneath the surface, dry mould; from 7 ft. to 16 ft., dry sandy mould; from 17 ft. to 38 ft., wet sand; and from 39 ft. to 45 ft., wet coarse sand.

The subsoil of Cairo is washed every year by the Nile, which brings to it in the summer the rain from the mountains of Abyssinia. In June the river at Cairo is at its lowest; then slowly begins to rise throughout July, and reaches its maximum flood in the first ten days of September, remaining high during September; and in October attains an artificial height, in consequence of the irrigation basins in Upper Egypt then allowing the water to escape and swirl on to complete the flood irrigation. During October the water gradually recedes from the basins, and is carried all over Lower Egypt by an elaborate system of canals, so that the early months of the year become gradually drier and drier, until the period of low Nile is again reached in May.

In the ordinary flood-time, there is considerable infiltration beneath the river-banks, besides the desired inundation for the future crops, so that the subsoil water rises in Cairo to a height of only 5 ft. from the ground surface, and at low Nile it sinks again to about 19 ft. below the surface. We may take it that during the winter season the subsoil water is more than 10 ft. from the ground.

Now, although subsoil drainage in England would seem to have resulted in an increase in the health of the population, and an especial diminution of phthisis and enteric fever, there is one practical good from this annual washing of the subsoil which must not be overlooked. For many years the resident population has allowed its filth to percolate into the porous soil and drain away as it pleased till it joined the level of subsoil water, and it is easy to conceive that if this earth were not periodically cleansed and oxygenated by the Nile infiltration, it would have long ceased to have any beneficial properties as a sponge. This cleansing process, which takes place in September and October, has, of course, the disadvantageous effect of altering the level, not only of the infiltrated soil water, but of the contents of all the uncemented cesspools of former and more insanitary days.

It must be borne in mind that the subsoil water has a slope of its own equal to that of the Delta, viz. 1 in 10,000, and, instead of remaining local, is constantly flowing northwards towards the sea. This is easily proved by experiments in this Delta or in India.

Sun, moon, and stars.—An average of eleven years taken from the Greenwich records tells us that there are in England only 1211 hours of bright sunshine during the twelve months, or less than two hours a day in the winter. It is unnecessary to take a similar observation at Cairo, but Table I. shows that we do have clouds during the cold months, in spite of an apparently perpetual sun-

Cairo.

shine. The sun is never too hot till the end of February for ladies, and men seldom require helmets till May. Indeed, some English officers have so little fear of the sun, that they wear all the year round no protection for their heads but the small red "fez." The maximum temperature in the sun at Cairo varies from 156° to 161° Fahr. in the summer. Twilight is, of course, almost absent from Cairo; but, on the other hand, in December, when the first chilly and cloudy days appear, the daylight is of three hours' longer duration than in England. The longest days are only fourteen hours with us, while the shortest are ten hours.

In nearly every village in Egypt there is a dance to the moon every month, dating from the days of Arab pagan moon-worship, but now incorporated into a dervish rite of the Mohammedan religion.

The moonlit nights at Cairo are very beautiful, and drives, rides, and dinner-parties at the Pyramids and elsewhere are very popular among the Europeans. The stillness and beauty of the desert at full moon are not easily forgotten. Owing to the clearness of the atmosphere, the moon has the appearance of being distinctly larger and nearer than in Europe; and the Gas Company of Cairo avails itself of a special clause in its contract, to the effect that at the time of full moon only four-fifths of the street-lamps need be lighted. When there is no moon, the star-spangled sky is a real treat, for the cloudy nights are few and far between, and the flat roofs of the houses easily lend themselves to the studies of amateur astronomers. Among the stars which can be seen in Cairo, but not in the latitudes of London, Boston, or Philadelphia, are Canopus and Horologium at the beginning of the year; while the Southern Cross shows about two-thirds of its height in May and June, though the foot of the cross cannot be seen till one goes south of Assouan. Ara and the Centaur are well seen in July, and the whole of the Scorpion shows to perfection; also at the close of the year we have the Crane and the Phœnix. The Milky Way is always beautiful, and the study of the stars has a special attraction in a country where one can become familiar with the original Arabic names still used by all those who have acquired the knowledge of the named stars.

It may be remembered that the march on Tel-el-Kebir, in 1882, before dawn, was steered by the stars, the English brigadiers being ordered to march on Arcturus.

Climate.—The isothermal line of Cairo runs between Algiers and St. Cruz, and between Florida and Canton (Pruner).

TABLE I.

| | Barometer. | Thermometer Fahr. | | | Humidity. | | Rain in inches. | Clouds 0—10. | Wind. | |
		Mean of maxima.	Mean of minima.	Mean of means.	Relative.	Absolute.			Direction.	Force in miles.
January ...	29·98	61·4	46·6	53·6	69·7	·28	·19	4·1	S.W.	2·2
February ...	29·95	65·3	48·8	57	66·2	·29	·24	4·2	N.	1·4
March ...	29·91	73·2	53	62·8	56·2	·29	·03	3·4	N.	2·5
April ...	29·82	81·2	59·9	70·4	47·8	·31	·12	3·4	N.	2·6
May ...	29·84	86·8	63·4	75·2	48·4	·38	·22	2·3	N.	2·8
June ...	29·78	94·7	70·2	82·6	44	·44	·02	1	N.	3
July ...	29·7	93	72·2	83·8	49	·5	—	1·2	N.	4·3
August ...	29·7	92·9	71·4	82·2	55·3	·51	—	1·6	N.	4·1
September...	29·83	87·5	68	77·8	62·1	·54	—	1·8	N.	4·3
October ...	29·89	84	64·8	74·3	65·8	·52	·21	2·5	N.	3·2
November ...	29·96	74·2	56·3	64·4	67·5	·39	·21	3	N.	2·1
December ...	29·99	67·7	50·4	58·4	69·6	·33	·19	3·7	N.	2·2
Average ...	29·86	80·1	60·4	70·2	58·46	·40	1·22	2·6	N.	2·9

Table I. is a resumé which I have made from the records of the five years 1884–88, the monthly bulletins being printed by the Khedivial Observatory in the Abbassiyeh suburb of Cairo.

The observations are taken throughout the day and night—at 6 a.m., 9 a.m, noon, 3 p.m., 6 p.m., 9 p.m., and midnight. The *barometer* used is a Fortin, verified and compared at Montsouris Observatory in Paris. The readings are reduced to freezing-point, and are taken at a level of 108·2 feet above the sea. My table shows that the variations are not very great, and its practical value is very little, though, as it falls when the wind changes to the south, and rises again when the prevailing north wind blows, it is useful to check the probable duration of a khamseen. The greatest variation during 1888 was 30·2 inches on one day in March, and 29·4 in. once in February. The *temperatures* are taken by a Centigrade thermometer, verified every year, and placed on a balcony thirty-two feet from the ground, facing north, and sheltered from the sun. The extremes of temperature are read daily from self-registering maximum and minimum instruments. The minimum result is generally found about 6 a.m. or a little earlier, and the daily maximum is invariably about 2 p.m. or 3 p.m.

During 1888, the absolute maximum reached

Cairo. 27

was 111·8° on July 13, while on the night of January 20, the absolute minimum of 36·4° was recorded. In 1887, the highest maximum was 110° on June 9, and the lowest minimum was 35·2° in January. Freezing-point seems never to be reached in Cairo; but a shallow dish of water placed in the wind on the ground in the desert, may be found occasionally with a thin coating of ice. I may say here, for the information of those who believe that Cairo is a furnace in the summer, that the *indoor* temperature of rooms on the north side of the house, kept properly shut during the hot hours, need never during the year exceed 83° Fahr.; and, on the other hand, that the same rooms, during the depths of winter, if properly opened to receive the warm outer air during the day, need never have a temperature below 52° Fahr., without employing a fire. By living in sunny south rooms, or by employing artificial heat, the invalid can be certain all night in the winter of a temperature of 65° Fahr., or more.

My observations, therefore, correspond with the results obtained by the Rev. Dr. Barnett in Cairo, which I give in Table II. For nearly two years he took observations six times daily, from 6 a.m. to 9 p.m., to ascertain the *indoor* temperature of an ordinary house.

His thermometers were hung between the windows in an inner room, on the second floor, with rooms above and all round, except on the east side, where there were two windows, on which the sun shone very little during the forenoon. The doors and windows were open in the night, but all closed at 9 a.m.

TABLE II.

	Maximum temperature of month.	Minimum temperature of month.	Mean daily range.
January	—	55°	5°
February	—	54°	5°
March	—	59°	5°
April	81·5°	70°	4°
May	86°	73°	3°
June	86°	79·5°	4°
July	87°	82°	2°
August	87·5°	82·5°	2·5°
September	85·5°	73°	2°
October	83°	69°	1·5°
November	75°	65°	2°
December	70°	63°	2·5°

The percentage of the *humidity* of the air is calculated by the usual tables from the readings of wet- and dry-bulb thermometers. The absolute humidity is the vapour-tension contained in the air, counted in inches of a column of mercury at freezing-point. The humidity of 58·4 may be compared with the mean annual humidity at

Greenwich, which is 87, or with 70·7, which is the record for Algiers in the year 1884.

But although Cairo is exceptionally dry, it has its damp moods at times, and several times a year for a few hours reaches saturation on the humidity scale. During the khamseen wind the percentage falls phenomenally low—to an absolute minimum of 4 on March 24, 1888, and once even to 3 per cent. in April, 1887.

Evaporation.—The quantity of water evaporated has been measured since 1887, and is obtained by means of a vessel containing water protected by coarse wire-gauze, and placed in the shade, but so that air can pass freely over it. The difference between the level of the water at any two observations gives the depth of water which has evaporated. The following are the numbers in inches for 1888, which was an average dry year;—January, 2·8; February, 2·8; March, 7·8; April, 7; May, 8·1; June, 11; July, 15·5; August, 12·3; September, 9·5; October, 7; November, 5; December, 4·4—total, 93·7 inches. For practical irrigation the evaporation in the basins is reckoned at 7 inches a month all through the year.

Rainfall.—Visitors sometimes come to Cairo believing that it never rains there, which is, however, almost true of Luxor. Table I. shows clearly that showers of rain are liable to fall during eight months of the year, though the total amount of the year is little more than one inch. This is always surprising to those who are accustomed to the averages of London, 24·7; Hyères, 28; Bournemouth, 28·9; Nice, 31·9; Algiers, 32; Torquay, 39·6; Pau, 43; Montreux, 50. At Cannes and Mentone, from November to April alone, the rainfall averages 32 and 17·8 inches respectively. The absence of rain and umbrellas does not necessarily make a country suitable for invalids, but it enables them to count with certainty upon the morrow being a fine day, and removes at least one element of risk and depression. Surface-drains for storm-water are not necessary in Cairo; the streets are watered by carts every day to prevent dust, and the trees often look as if it would be a charity to wash their leaves.

Dew.—A small amount of dew is always present in Cairo and the desert on account of the great difference in temperature between that of the day and night. (M. Barbey found ninety-three grammes on a square metre of mackintosh at Ismailia in March, 1880.)

The temperature of the Nile water is a little higher in the early morning than the temperature of the air, and therefore a line of mist can be sometimes seen early in the day during December and January, which accurately marks out the line of the river. The annual regularity of the rise and fall of temperature, of the barometer and of humidity, of the wind, of sunshine, and of the Nile flood are elements which materially combine to ensure the comfort of the invalid visitor. It is easy for any intelligent resident to be "weather wise," and to prophesy for his friends the condition of the immediate future.

During 1887 there were showers of rain on fifteen days. Thunder and lightning occur about once a year, and hail is rather less common, while snow is unknown. The May rainfall in my table is exceptionally high in consequence of an abnormal storm in 1887.

The state of the sky is judged by figures running from 0 to 10, and shows an excellent average. The clouds are brought up from the sea by the north wind, or the sky becomes overcast during a south wind from the infinitesimal particles of sand which seem to be held in suspension in the air.

Wind.—The prevailing wind both in Cairo and Alexandria is always from the north, though it may be noticed that a cool dry wind blows from the desert during January. Also one sees that the force of the wind, which is calculated by means of an anemometer, and shows the number of miles per hour, is abated during the winter months, and only becomes freshened when the summer has set in. Two miles per hour is usually reckoned "calm," five miles is considered "light air," ten miles "light breeze," and 41·4, which was the maximum wind-velocity during 1888, is called "moderate gale."

The khamseen wind is the only bad one in Egypt. It is so called, not because it lasts for fifty days, but because it is liable to occur during the fifty days which follow Easter Monday, and possibly has some connection with the equinoctial gales elsewhere. It blows from the south or south-south-east, the more easterly variety being the most disagreeable. It usually continues three days, but may in rare cases last as many as seven days. The number of khamseen days in any one year would seem to vary from four to twenty. We wake in the morning to find a great calm, clouded sky, grey atmosphere, and an invisibly fine sand suspended in the air, which seems to have been caught up from the desert and to be held there until the wind veers again to the north at sunset on the third day, and the air becomes once more clear, cool, and even cold. On a really bad day the sun's rays are wholly obscured, and the atmosphere becomes intensely dry, and approaches the colour of a London yellow fog. It finishes with a conflict of the winds overhead until the north gains the day, and with the fall sometimes of a few drops of rain; after this a refreshing north breeze blows again for a week or ten days, and then the khamseen may again appear.

Russegger is quoted as having proved that a quantity of free electricity is found in the air during a khamseen, at first negative, afterwards positive, and then rapidly changing from one to the other. This question is worthy of study, for no intelligent man can undergo the odd experience of this wind without being certain that some unusual electrical disturbance is taking place.

The consideration of the effect of this disturbance upon invalids is very important, and it may at once be said that they do not seem to suffer more than the rest of the Europeans, and even in many cases suffer less, because, unlike their more robust associates, they are not suddenly debarred by the rapid rise of thermometer from taking active exercise. The fall of temperature at the end of three days' dry heat is apt to be more dangerous to imprudent people than the heat itself, for in March there may be upon these days a fall of 30° Fahr. at sunset. The general effects of the khamseen are a little excitement and stimulation of the system, a more rapid succession of ideas and increased action of some of the functions, followed by listlessness, headache, and languor. Some warmth-loving Europeans actually luxuriate in a mild khamseen; but all others are seriously inconvenienced by not being able to pursue their ordinary outdoor life, and those whose work does not permit of their resting feel fagged and tired before the close of the day. The effect on natives would seem to be something similar, the street-occupants lying about in all positions on the paths, instead of sitting and chattering as on other days. Fever patients in bed do not seem to be conscious of the change to khamseen weather. Bronchitic and phthisical individuals are rather benefited than otherwise by the dry, warm air; but it is doubtful whether the air would not be too stimulating for those with a tendency to hæmoptysis.

My only experience on this point is derived from one young Englishwoman, whose expectoration in March became a little bloody. She liked the khamseen days; but I thought it prudent to send her to Ramleh, chiefly because she had a very bad family history of hæmoptysis. A bad khamseen, besides its effects on the human race, shrivels up roses and other flowers, and will even warp and crack unseasoned wood. It is curious that the same southerly wind, so hot in March and April, is occasionally in winter the coldest that blows, the difference being that then the sun's rays fall more obliquely on the desert, and the wind is chilled by its passage over the mountains of Abyssinia.

After April the Cairo temperature is always above 70° Fahr., and invalids are glad to hurry away through the gates of Europe, which are no longer closed against them. Rheumatism and lung cases which are in need of "sun-bathing" can and do stay till May and June, and the few phthisical patients who have remained in Egypt all the year round have not regretted it so far as we know. It is only natural that Europeans should wish to leave Egypt for their own homes directly the heat becomes markedly felt; but every spring we have the same experience of patients writing back to us of the cheerlessness and cold in some spot less favoured than sunny, rainless Cairo.

Has the climate of Cairo changed during recent years or not? Modern visitors are always told by travellers of an earlier generation that the climate has woefully depreciated, and has lost its charm of dryness because of the improvements in irrigation, and of the trees and gardens which have sprung into being since 1850.

Let us examine the few broken records of the climate that we possess and compare them with Table I. But before we make this modern comparison, let us remember that we have no grounds for supposing that during historic times has there been any appreciable change in the rainfall, the river-flow, or the sand-blow of the country. There is said to be only one evidence on the monuments of rain having been known in Lower Egypt, and we see around us to-day the mud-brick tombs covered with stucco, dating from the Third or Fourth Dynasty (B.C. 3800), when they were built without any apparent fear of their dissolution.

First, let us take the number of days on which rain fell in any one year in Cairo :—

1798–1800	15 days.
1835–39	12 ,,
1857–61	13 ,,
1871	9 ,,
1887	15 ,,

This shows no perceptible difference; but the annual rainfall for 1835–39 (Destrouches) is said to have averaged less than half an inch, and if so, we now have almost three times more rain than formerly.

The following table shows a comparison of mean temperatures at Cairo, taken at intervals during the last hundred and twenty-eight years, but not always at similar hours, which probably accounts for the variation shown in column 4. The net result shows no decided change in the regularity of Cairo temperature.

TABLE III.

	*1761-2.	†1799-1801.	‡1835-9.	§1868-73.	‖1884-8.
January	56·2	56	—	56·8	53·6
February	58	57·2	—	62·2	57
March	66·6	63·5	—	70·6	62·8
April	69·8	72	—	78·4	70·4
May	77·9	75·8	—	84	75·2
June	82·1	83·5	—	85·4	82·6
July	85·2	86·4	—	83·6	83·8
August	87·3	84·2	—	79·6	82·2
September	—	74	—	73·4	77·8
October	—	73	—	65·8	74·3
November	66	65·9	—	58·8	64·4
December	58·6	61·2	—	55·2	58·3
Average	70·7	71	70·2	71·2	70·2

* M. Niebuhr (Pruner). † Description de l'Egypte.
‡ Dr. Destouches (Patterson). § Klima der Mittelmeerländer, 1879.
‖ From my Table I.

For the sake of those who do not want to be troubled with tables of figures, I have made a practical analysis of the several months at Cairo, and to this have added the arrivals of migratory birds for the sportsman, and the approximate dates when ripe fruit and flowers first appear in the gardens. Much, of course, might be written on the agricultural produce of a medium country which assimilates barley from the north and bananas from the south in the same way as it embraces individuals from all parts of the world.

October.—Resident European families return to

Cairo after the middle of the month, because the summer is then rather suddenly at an end, and winter clothing is issued to the troops. But the proportion of heat to dampness is still great, mosquitoes are rampant, and invalids are not advised to arrive till the last days of the month at the very earliest. Quail are already in Upper Egypt, and snipe, ducks, and geese are arriving. Fresh dates are at their best, grapes, and custard-apples. Bananas have begun, and continue all the winter. Among flowers there are dahlia, zinnia, periwinkle, and tuberoses.

November.—A beautiful month for invalids to arrive, and before the crush of pleasure-seekers, so that good rooms can be easily secured. The Nile inundation is still out between the town and the Pyramids, and the sunsets are perhaps more beautiful than at any other time of year. Weather no longer too hot for outdoor exercise. Mosquitoes disappearing, though nets are always wanted at night throughout the year, and fair-skinned strangers suffer until they become acclimatized. Oranges and lemons. Chrysanthemums and lovely pointsettia shrubs.

December.—At the end of the month we are liable to a little cloud and rain, and invalids who want to avoid all cold damp should go up to Luxor. Temperature like a dry September in England.

Starlings arrive. Oranges and lemons again, as in all the winter months. Balsam and heliotrope.

January.—There is often a cold south wind from the desert, and though the days are not really cold, the evenings require a fire indoors and an overcoat abroad. Lung invalids ought not to be out after sunset. Temperature like the last week of September in England. Quail return to Upper Egypt from the Soudan. Roses bloom all the year round in Cairo, but they are now at their best. Hyacinth, camellia, mignonette, ranunculus, cyclamen, verbena, gypsophila, and orange-flowers.

February.—Temperature like a dry English September, chilly at the beginning of the month, but warm and pleasant at the end, so that fires and overcoats are hardly wanted at night. Invalids return from Luxor to Cairo at the end of February to escape the south winds, which begin earlier there. Quail breed in Upper Egypt, and appear again in Lower Egypt; starlings take their flight. Oranges, lemons, and loquats. Violets, petunias, phlox, bougainvillia, and roses.

March.—Temperature is a little like London in July, but the great feature of this month is the south wind, which is almost certain to blow at least twice for two or three days at a time. It is at first welcomed as a pleasant change after the cold weather, but soon becomes disagreeable. The last week of the month is often hot, but previous to that, during a south wind, the shade temperature at noon is about 80°; indoors it is 64°; the barometer falls from 30 to 29·7, and there are 10° difference between the wet and dry bulbs. Tourists tire of Egypt at the first hot wind, and make for Palestine, Constantinople, etc. Snipe, ducks, and geese leave for Europe; excellent quail, spur-winged plover, and dove shooting. Dianthus, pansy, China aster, marguerites, delphinium, fuchsia, gladiolus, lobelia, sweet pea, and wall-flowers. Acacia trees in the boulevards shed their leaves and remain bare for about a month.

April.—The days are warm like the hottest days in an English summer, but are not felt so oppressive because of the dryness of the air. The houses and habits of the country are also specially adapted for the hot weather. Rooms are now occupied which face towards the north and catch the cool wind, and on hot days it is wisest not to go out immediately after luncheon. European houses and hotels are built so that the rooms are sixteen feet high, thus providing for plenty of cubic space when the windows are obliged to be closed to keep out the heat and the flies and mosquitoes, which now begin to be troublesome. The khamseen wind occurs at intervals of about ten days, and great care ought to be taken not to relinquish all winter clothing, though the temperature is often above 90° Fahr. for a few hours at a time. Invalids leave for Ramleh, or for Italy and the south of France. Strawberries and apricots. Oleander, pelargonium, and sunflowers.

May.—We are still liable to occasional khamseen winds, and each week the weather is becoming warmer; but Cairo is now very lovely; the trees in the streets have their new foliage, and the gardens are bright with many subtropical flowering trees and shrubs. On May 6 I once saw the exceptional event of a thunder and lightning storm, with hailstones as big as dried peas, and a shade temperature of 85° Fahr. Quail leave Egypt for Europe. Sweet melons and water-melons. Balsam, magnolia, lotus, jessamine, convolvulus, and passionflowers.

June, July, August.—These are the three hottest months of the year, and in August the climate is already becoming a little damp in consequence of the rising Nile. Rich natives spend these months in Alexandria, Syria, or Constantinople. Europeans in Cairo take a siesta after luncheon. Government offices are closed at 1 p.m., but after 4 p.m. every Englishman goes out to ride, drive, golf, or lawn-tennis, and the British soldier plays cricket and football. The nights are always cool, so that it is possible to dine out of doors without insects, and afterwards to sleep well. The families of European officials usually leave for Europe at the beginning of June, but some ladies only leave Egypt every other summer. Sand-grouse and *bec figues* (fig-eaters). Grapes, almonds, peaches, figs, and melons in June; and in August, in addition, there are mangoes, dates, and custard-apples. Dahlias, zinnias, periwinkle, tuberoses, and the perennial hibiscus.

September.—This is a hot, damp month, the most trying of the year. The temperature is decidedly lower than in the three preceding months, and there is no rain; but the Nile flood and inundation produce a state of dampness which, together with the comparative heat, is trying for Europeans. Judged by the thermometer alone, the month is not unlike May in Cairo, but the raising of the humidity from 48 to 62 per cent. makes all the difference. Grey quail reach Egypt. Cotton-picking begins. Prickly pears, bananas, and summer fruits and flowers.

CHAPTER IV.

CAIRO—(*continued*).

Public health in Cairo.—There has been no census since 1882, and it is doubtful whether the statistics then gathered are sufficiently accurate. There are believed to be about 375,000 inhabitants, of whom 21,650 are not Turkish subjects, and are mostly Europeans. The deaths among Europeans during the last seven years, including the cholera year, have averaged 473, or 21·8 per 1000 per annum, which compares favourably with any town in Europe or America. But the figures ought probably to be higher, as it is difficult to conceive that the lowest classes of Maltese, Jews, Greeks, and Levantines, who are all included among the foreigners, must not considerably deteriorate the mortality rate. The death-rate among the natives is shockingly high, 46·5 per 1000, and this is principally due to the mortality (800 a month) of infants under one year of age during the four hottest months of the year, diarrhœa being the most common certified cause of death. Those unacquainted with the lowest class of Egyptians can form no idea of the filth in which they voluntarily live, of the habits of the nursing mothers, and of their indifference to medical aid until the child is actually dead. The apathy of the people on this subject is perhaps partly due to the extraordinarily high birth-rate among the natives. The average birth-rate in Cairo during the last six years is 51·8, and that of Alexandria is 48·5 per 1000. During 1887 the highest birth-rate recorded per 1000 among ninety-five other towns publishing vital statistics were — Dusseldorf, 39·1; Buenos Ayres, 39·7; Chemnitz, 44·8: while the figures for Egyptian towns were—Suez and Ismailia, 54·2; Cairo, 55·4; Alexandria, 57·9; and Port Said, 73·7. It is melancholy to reflect that one-third of the native children die before they have lived twelve months, and more than one-half of them die before they have reached the age of five years. It is doubtful whether this extraordinary fecundity extends itself to European residents in Egypt, whose habits and laws of divorce are, of course, entirely different. During my own residence in Cairo, I have known thirty-five English brides (æt. 20–35) who have been imported into Egypt; of these twenty-seven have borne one or more children, one died shortly after marriage, and the remaining seven are as yet childless.

It will be interesting to note what diseases visitors to Egypt are likely to suffer from during their stay.

First and most frequent comes Diarrhœa, which seems to be invariably produced by a chill, such as cold after a sunny day, and possibly by neglecting to wear a flannel belt round the waist by day or night, which seems to be a good preventive. The individual seems to be attacked, as he might be in Europe, by a " cold in the head "—is probably fatigued by exertion at the time, and eats an ordinary meal afterwards. In the early morning he is awakened by mild diarrhœa, which continues two or three days, and readily yields to rest, milk diet, gentle aperients, and bismuth. Less mild cases occur in delicate women, which seem to be due to congestion of the intestine—are associated with mild fever for three days, and are cured in about a week. I have never been able to trace any case to the drinking-water, and it occurs among those who filter, boil, and filter again their water. Some strong robust men laugh at flannel belts and never wear them, but to weaker vessels they are a great comfort and useful preventive of catarrh.

Dysentery I have only seen three times in six

years among visitors, and three times among resident Europeans who had previously suffered from the disease in other countries. All were mild cases, and yielded readily to saline aperients and astringents, or ipecacuanha.

Of more than twenty cases of Enteric fever which I have had to treat among the English and Americans, only nine have occurred amongst the visitors, and all recovered, and of these nine six were ill of the disease when they arrived in Cairo, having contracted it in Palestine (two), Naples (two), Luxor, and during a Nile voyage. Of the three remaining cases, one young lady had the fever in 1883, when Cairo was much more insanitary than it is to-day; a second caught it in 1888, while living against medical advice in a house where there was no pretence of sanitation; and the third was the English maid of the second, who sickened after she and her mistress had been removed to a clean house. After making careful inquiry of my sanitary and medical colleagues, I have not been able to hear of any case of enteric among European civilians during the winter of 1888-9, excepting a few cases all imported from elsewhere.

Cholera visited Egypt in 1865 and in 1883, but not since, and the theory that it was endemic in the country has not been borne out by late experience.

Cairo.

Dengue fever was present in 1880 and 1887, but only from August to November: it is a painful malady, without danger to life. Typhus and relapsing fevers occur in the spring among overcrowded natives, but no case has been known among Europeans. The plague left Egypt, we hope for ever, in 1844. Small-pox, as in other parts of the world, is liable to occur among those insufficiently protected by vaccination, but I remember only one case of a visitor and one of a resident. The deaths from small-pox in Cairo for 1886-7-8, have averaged forty. Measles occasionally occurs as an epidemic among the natives, and causes many deaths; but I know of no visitors who have caught the disease, and only a dozen residents. Rötheln I have not yet heard of in Egypt. Scarlatina is so rare that it is only heard of at very rare intervals among the British troops. Diphtheria is not uncommon among native children, and every now and then attacks Europeans who live in insanitary houses. Whooping-cough is almost unknown, mumps very rare, and the ordinary influenza catarrh of England is uncommon. Congestion of the liver is more likely to attack alcoholic residents than visitors, and both classes are liable to pleurisy or pneumonia, if they persist in imprudent exposure at night. Phthisis does not occur among white residents, though, on the other hand, there are plenty of doctors and others in Cairo who came to the country as confirmed consumptives, and are now hard-working and apparently healthy members of the community. The disease attacks blacks, who are, of course, living as foreigners in a cold northern latitude; and those of the Egyptians who are saturated by scrofula or syphilis may fall a prey to it.

Malaria is almost non-existent in Cairo, and this is the more wonderful because many of the causes in other countries would seem to be present. During September and October those living on the river-banks are liable to contract mild intermittent or simple continued fever, but at other times of the year even those who have suffered in India and elsewhere are free of malarious attacks.

Ophthalmia in its granular form I have never seen among any visitors or among English residents who are ordinarily careful of their eyes; the catarrhal ophthalmia occurs among many who live in the country, and is troublesome when the winds laden with imperceptibly fine dust are blowing. The best protection is to wear gauze goggles to keep out the glare and dust, to use a saturated solution of boracic acid to wash the eyes as a toilet requisite, and to employ, when necessary, weak collyria of sulphate of zinc.

Those who persistently drink muddy water are

liable to become the hosts of various entozoa. Sunstroke even in its slightest forms can only be obtained on exceptional days by some great imprudence on the part of the individual.

Water-supply.—All Egyptian towns get their drinking-water direct from the Nile, or indirectly from the canals fed by the Nile. The Cairo Water Company, which has a complete monopoly for many years, has lately, under pressure from the Sanitary Department, made some important improvements in the supply. The intake is now from the Nile itself, but used to be from a canal, which during the summer months was liable to become stagnant; it has been proposed to remove the intake some four miles higher up the river, above all source of contamination. The water is pumped to the filter-beds at Abbassiyeh, whence, after filtration, it returns to the town for consumption; all the European quarters are now supplied with filtered water, the daily average being about 26,000 cubic metres. The velocity of the river at high Nile is about five feet a second, or nearly three and a half miles an hour; but at low Nile, the velocity is reduced to at least one-fifth of this.

The filter-beds are on raised ground in the desert, and consist, in the first place, of two huge tanks, into which the water is always flowing; from these it is admitted into eight filter-beds, each of about 2700 square yards, and after filtration it is received into two closed reservoirs. The filters are 2 ft. 4 in. deep, and consist of sand, different sizes of gravel and stones, which come from the Red Hill at Abbassiyeh, before mentioned. The sand is pure white, from a pit between a pretty stratum of conglomerate travertine and a lower layer of conglomerate pebble, and is far removed from all danger arising from the neighbourhood of old cemeteries. The place for getting the sand had to be changed two years ago, because the workmen discovered they were near the dry osseous remains of an unknown mediæval burying-place. The sand is all washed before being used, and the superficial layers of the beds are removed every four days in the summer, and every eight days in the winter, when the water is less thick. The deep layers of the beds are only changed two or three times a year, which is probably not often enough. The beds and plant are under the constant inspection of the Sanitary Department, who have also made some interesting analyses of the filtered Nile water. Table IV. shows the results of twenty-three analyses made during twelve months, by Mr. F. E. Pollard, F.I.C., F.C.S., who has made a speciality of the subject.

The samples were taken in mid-stream, one yard below the surface, and about one hundred yards north of Kasr-el-Nil bridge, near the Company's intake.

Cairo.

TABLE IV.

Sample taken.	Parts per million.			Grains per gallon.			Hardness Wanklyn's scale.	Grains per gallon.
	Free ammonia.	Albuminoid ammonia.	Oxygen absorbed in ten minutes.	Total solids at 150° C.	Chlorine.	Nitrates as N_2O_5.		Suspended matter in unfiltered water.
1888.								
July 7	—	·2	3	20·44	2·1	·016	—	·98
July 21	·03	·2	2·2	16·38	1·35	·022	—	4·2
August 4	·08	·17	2·8	14·21	1·05	·022	—	29·96
August 20	·048	·065	3	10·01	·4	·266	—	116·13
September 1	·07	·1	3·2	9·59	·25	·222	—	161·84
September 22	·044	·11	2·3	8·96	·2	·133	—	114·52
October 6	·026	·115	2·05	8·54	·2	·133	5·7	73·02
October 20	·01	·1	2·2	8·75	·18	·155	5·8	64·75
November 3	—	·2	2·5	9·59	·17	·133	6·2	56·91
November 17	·01	·07	2·9	8·68	·25	·155	6·1	33·81
December 8	·01	·06	2·2	8·82	·2	·122	6·3	18·34
December 22	—	·08	2·8	9·52	·2	·077	6·1	14·63
1889.								
January 5	—	·1	3·2	9·24	·25	·072	6·2	9·52
January 19	·018	·1	3·3	9·8	·35	·094	5·9	8·96
February 2	—	·09	2·95	10·64	·5	·033	6·2	7·14
February 16	·01	·1	2·8	12·11	·8	·027	6·3	6·09
March 2	—	·1	2·8	13·65	1	·026	6·9	4·2
March 16	·01	·11	3·2	14·14	1·25	·022	8·2	3·5
April 6	—	·12	2·9	16·11	1·55	·044	8·7	4·13
April 20	—	·11	2·7	18·06	1·85	·038	8·7	2·8
May 4	·01	·11	2·8	18·45	2·1	·044	8·9	2·24
May 18	·01	·11	2·9	20·3	2·4	·055	8·9	1·19
June 8	·02	·16	2·7	19·81	2·8	·066	8·9	2·31
Average	·017	·116	2·7	12·86	·93	·086	7	32·26
Winter average	·005	·104	2·85	12·8	·92	·067	7·1	12·39
New River	·012	·066	2·48	17·6	1·1	·94	15	

The water, when filtered through double paper, is perfectly clear, and has a greyish yellow colour, varying in depth, but always to be observed in thin glass vessels. Its taste is usually considered very agreeable, and the Arabs have a proverb that he who once drinks it becomes enamoured of Egypt. At the foot of the table I have made a comparison between the average water of the year, the average of the winter months (November 3 to May 18)—which is seen to be much less thick before filtered, and a little purer than the year's average after filtration—and also the water of the New River Company which supplies the north of London and the City, and is purer than that furnished by the Thames Companies. It will be seen that the Cairo water compares satisfactorily with that of London.

The amount of oxygen absorbed was determined by the French official process. The amount of chlorine varies very considerably, and this has already been pointed out by Professor Wanklyn,[*] who explains the variability by saying that the storm-water of the flood sweeps over the surface of ground long ago denuded of salt, and therefore furnishing but little chlorine. On the other hand, when the river has fallen, it receives water which has passed deeper into the ground, and which has

[*] "Water Analysis," 1879, p. 152.

Cairo.

undergone concentration by evaporation, besides having washed the lower strata, from which it extracts chlorine.

As a confirmation of this, we see that the chlorine is at its maximum just before the annual flood.

The deficiency of nitrates is interesting, but does not necessarily show an absence of defilement. The softness of the water makes it very agreeable for all domestic purposes; the slight variation in hardness is due to carbonate of lime, through which the river has cut its way. The analyses of 1888-9 showed a trace of iron, but of no poisonous metals, and no nitrites, and Heisch's sewage test never gave the slightest evidence of sewage contamination.

The unfiltered water should never be drunk by visitors or residents, though the natives prefer it infinitely. Some imprudent tourists drink it from the dirty porous jars of the villagers, and must not wonder at suffering occasionally in consequence.

The suspended matter, which is the chief fertilizing ingredient of the Nile, varies in quantity in the most wonderful way. Mr. Pollard's figures vary from ·9 in July, to 161·8 in September, while Dr. Letheby found 3·3 in May, 1875, and 104·4 grains in August, 1874. The fertility of the flood, besides the clay, is due to the organic matter, and to the salts of potash and phosphoric acid dissolved and suspended in it. I should add that a very laudatory report on the Cairo Company's water, was made in 1889, by Professor Müntz, of the National Agricultural Institute of Paris.

The following is an analysis of the solids in Nile water taken on October 6, 1888, with the probable chemical combinations (Pollard):—

Calcic carbonate	3·521	grains per gallon.
Magnesic carbonate	1·421	,, ,,
Silica	1·33	,, ,,
Sodic sulphate	·791	,, ,,
Potassic sulphate	·469	,, ,,
Sodic carbonate	·434	,, ,,
Sodic chloride	·322	,, ,,
Potassic nitrate	·245	,, ,,
Ferric and aluminic oxides	·063	,, ,,
	8·596	

The water, before being drunk in Cairo, is passed through large earthenware jars, which are found in every house, and constitute an excellent filter, removing every trace of colour and cloudiness and all deposit, after the water has been allowed to stand for twenty-four hours. Drinking-water is further poured into porous vessels, where it is kept deliciously cool, and gains an agreeable taste. Charcoal filters and boiling are not necessary, but there is no difficulty about carrying this out, if desired.

Most of the ice bought in Cairo is made from the filtered water by the Water Company.

Scavenging.—Before 1885 it was only the streets of the European quarters that were cleaned, and this work was done at shameful expense by a contractor employed by the Governor of Cairo. Now the work is well done by the Sanitary Department all over the town, and at a less cost than before. All streets are kept swept, the made roads are watered by carts every day, and the narrow lanes in the native quarters are watered by the inhabitants with goat-skins. Up till 7 a.m. the householders are allowed to deposit in the street in heaps their dry refuse, which is collected in carts, and either burnt in the Turkish baths or shot outside the town. This successfully prevents all the dust-bin nuisances, and is very important in an Oriental country where women and children seldom leave the house, and are unprovided in the poorest cases with water-closets.

Cesspools and drains.—A few English residents have nothing but earth-closets in their houses; others have, during my own sanitary knowledge of the country, established cemented cesspools, which are carefully trapped and ventilated, and from which the fæcal matter and urine are removed by an odourless pneumatic system (Tallard) by night. To this category belong all the hotels and houses which one can safely recommend, and under existing circumstances this is the best arrangement that can be made to protect householders from the chance of being poisoned by their neighbours. It is satisfactory to those of us who have laboured for sanitary reform to know that all individual houses and hotels protected with care have escaped such diseases as enteric and diphtheria, and, moreover, are less troubled by mosquitoes, which are baffled by the syphon traps. But, unfortunately, the bulk of Cairo, and most of the mosques which act as public latrines, are provided with uncemented cesspools, draining into the porous earth for most of the year, and becoming dangerously filled by the high Nile in summer, and it is this which demands urgent reform.

Happily, the European quarters of the town are quite modern, and the soil has not yet had time to become saturated with sewage, and the native parts have only quite recently obtained a supply of water.

The capitulations protecting all Europeans, and the apathy and ignorance of the native Government, have hitherto prevented any radical measures being taken; but in 1889 the Government employed Mr. Baldwin Latham to thoroughly examine the sanitary condition of Cairo, and to report upon what steps should be taken to improve it. This is a great step in the right direction, and it is confidently hoped that money may at once be found for carrying out these reforms.

Until then individuals must continue to protect themselves by cutting off all communication with the ground, and by carefully trapping and ventilating all pipes.

In the mean time, all street-sewers have been blocked and destroyed, because they are unnecessary for storm water, and because it was found that house proprietors used them as overflows for their cesspools, and thus vitiated the fresh air of the streets. At the same time some gaspipes, which were too small, made of zinc, and allowed leakage in the surrounding earth, and consequent odour, have been removed, and replaced by six-inch iron pipes, which are a great improvement. All cesspools are now prevented from draining into the Nile or canals, and are obliged to be emptied at least every six months, those of the cemented type of course requiring to be emptied much oftener. The sewage is taken in patent shut carts to Abbassiyeh desert by night, at the rate of over 30,000 tons a year. There it is deodorized and sifted, and sold to the fellaheen as "poudrette" at £2 a ton for use on their lands. These changes, though not nearly radical enough, have already contributed greatly to the comfort and health of the European inhabitants.

Hotels.—The following is a list of the principal hotels in Cairo, in the order of their available accommodation, but not necessarily in order of merit. The prices are for one bedroom per day, but they are all capable of reduction if the visitor proposes a long stay. Private sitting-rooms are an extra charge.

New—16s.; 175 bedrooms (some new in 1889); electric lighting; excellent position; pays a rental annually of nearly £4000; could be made perfectly sanitary with ease; fireplaces.

Shepheard's—16s.; 150 bedrooms (a few new with balconies in 1889); electric bells; fireplaces; and many modern improvements to please the English; lawn-tennis court; smoking-room and ladies' sitting-room; garden; new cesspools, carefully cemented and trapped.

Oriental—10s.; 80 beds.

Continental—14s.; 75 beds; opened in November, 1889; cesspools cemented, etc.

D'Angleterre—12s.; 65 beds; clients almost exclusively English; cesspools cemented at sides, but not on their floors.

Royal—12s.; 65 beds.

Khedivial—10s.; 58 beds.

Victoria—12s.; 53 bedrooms in three detached houses in a pretty rose-garden; clients all English and American; two cemented and two uncemented cesspools.

Du Nil—12s. ; 50 beds ; clients mostly German; is in a bad neighbourhood, but much frequented by artists and others who want to be near the native quarters.

All the above hotels have taken some pains about sanitary improvements during the last six years, and those which specially desire the English custom are now in fairly good order, but some of the others retain as yet their old system. In none of the above hotels has there been any case of enteric fever arising in Cairo itself during the season of 1888–9. There are, of course, several smaller hotels which I have not here mentioned.

Pensions.—Of these again there are several, two of which may be mentioned : *Ismailieh*—13s. ; 40 beds ; three private sitting-rooms ; two general sitting-rooms ; piano, etc. ; baths ; douches ; gymnastic apparatus, etc. ; much frequented by the English. *Couteret*—10s. ; 30 beds.

Lodgings, furnished and unfurnished, can be obtained during the season, but they are either very expensive or not very good, as all rents are very high in Cairo. Moreover, visitors outside a hotel may find it difficult to have servants who do not talk their language easily.

Clubs.—There are two excellent clubs, at one of which there are some residential chambers for temporary members.

Carriages.—The ordinary street carriage is a comfortable two-horsed Victoria at a modest tariff. There are landaus for those who wish them, and also broughams for going out at night. The roads are wide and good, and shaded better than almost any other city with avenues of acacia (*Albizzia lebbek*), so that carriage-exercise is rendered very easy and agreeable.

Riding.—Excellent country-bred and Syrian ponies can be hired by the day, but a visitor intending to spend the winter generally does better to buy a mount for £18 or £25. Donkey-riding is very cheap, very healthy, and at times enjoyable. Camels can be obtained for the desert, but are out of place in crowded streets rendered slippery by watering.

Doctors.—Commencing with our own countrymen, there are two Aberdonians, who have been respectively twenty-seven and nine years in Egypt, and a Londoner, who has practised in Cairo for six years. There is another Englishman who practises chiefly among the natives, and has a growing surgical reputation; six English doctors in the Government service are available for consultation; and there are always a similar number in the English Army. There are German, Scotch, and American oculists, a good English dentist, and more than a dozen foreign medical men (some speaking English), who are held in the highest repute among their various colonies.

There are good rubbers of both sexes, and some trustworthy chemists accustomed to English prescriptions.

Nurses.—Besides foreign nurses, there are three Englishwomen trained in English hospitals available for private cases, and there is now a Nursing institution in connection with the native hospital, from which two or three English ladies trained in London hospitals may be obtained on application to the secretary.

Churches.—The English Protestant church was opened in 1876, and has lately been enlarged. The English colony is fortunate in possessing a very popular chaplain, who is beloved by all. There are two Roman Catholic churches, a German Lutheran, an American Presbyterian, and many Greek and Coptic places of worship.

Shops.—Shopping is now very easy in Cairo, because, in addition to a few English shops, at all good establishments there are men who talk English or French, and all civilized requisites at a fixed price can now be obtained. The native bazaars are a constant source of enjoyment to residents and visitors, and the only objection to them is that some of them are near insanitary houses.

Library.—Besides booksellers in the town, there is a very good circulating library with more than two thousand popular works, including many relating to Egypt. This is a recent improvement, and greatly appreciated by travellers.

Hospitals.—Paying patients are received at a German and at an Austrian hospital, but the former is generally patronized by the English who desire hospital treatment and the kind nursing of Kaiserwerth deaconesses. The female wards of the native hospital for free patients are now under English management, and can sometimes be visited by special permission.

Theatres.—Cairo boasts of a very pretty opera-house, with a splendid stage, for which Verdi wrote "Aida" in the days of the late Khedive's extravagance. It is generally hired during the winter months by a French or Italian Company, and at other times by travelling actors, among whom have been Sarah Bernhardt and M. Coquelin. At a second theatre there is often Italian comedy to be seen, and a wandering circus visits us every year.

The *Ezbekieh Gardens* are named after a mosque built by the Emir Ezbeky, a general of Kait Bey in 1486, and destroyed to make room for the Court of Mixed Tribunals. A desolate piece of swampy ground was in 1870 converted into a picturesque garden of twenty and a half acres by the landscape gardener to whom Paris owes the Bois de Boulogne. The gardens are skilfully laid out, and, being close to the hotels, are a useful resort by day for those who cannot take active exercise; but after sunset they are liable to be damp, in consequence of the perpetual watering of the ground and the presence of a small lake. Grass grows with difficulty in Cairo, and the *Lippia nodiflora* is made to take its place. There is a good restaurant, which is in great request during the summer, when military bands play in the gardens after dinner. There are very few trees or shrubs with which we are familiar in English gardens, but ivy may be seen with the cactus clinging to stately palms. Australia has furnished the she-oak and the beef-wood tree; there are sparmannia from the Cape of Good Hope; and from South America, clumps of cocos trees, silk cotton trees, and habrothamnus. Among the most noticeable trees are the blue flowering *Jacaranda mimosifolia,* the *Erythrina cristogalli,* and the pepper-tree from Brazil; the lovely orange-red flowering flamboyant (*Pointciana regia*) from Madagascar, which is now planted in some of the Cairo streets; the mossy-cupped oak from Constantinople; the Malabar nut, frangipanni, red bean tree, and pudding-pipe tree from India; the rice paper and the *Hibiscus rosasmensis* from China; the *Cæsalpinia Gilliesii* of Peru; and the sacred tree of Nubia (*Kigiela pinnata*). Many of the trees have now been labelled, and among them may be found the Norfolk Island pine, Indian beech, *Yucca gloriosa*, twenty different kinds of figs, the India horse-chestnut, the *Acacia farnesiana*, and towering indiarubber trees. Then one sees also tropical sedge, oleanders which are bright with all colours in April and May, and many commoner varieties too numerous to mention. Here and there in the garden are solitary giants of the *Albizzia lebbek*, which was introduced into Egypt one hundred and fifty years ago, and, besides making beautiful avenues in Cairo, has now spread all over the country. It grows with great rapidity and with extraordinary ease, and requires no watering after the first few years. Unfortunately it has lately been attacked by the larva of a beetle, and some of the oldest trees have died in consequence.

Flora.—Almost the only strictly indigenous trees in Egypt are the tamarisk, the sunt (*Acacia Nilotica*), and the sycamore-fig, but the flora consist of about 1400 specimens. Among the many successfully introduced trees is the Jerusalem thorn (*Parkinsonia aculeata*), which flourishes especially in the desert at Abbassiyeh and Helouan. The lotus is found in Cairo in the spring, but is rather rare, and the papyrus is no longer a native of Egypt. Dr. Schweinfurth believes that the Egyptian oases were colonized by Berbers with the cereals of the Mediterranean basin, but that the valley of the Nile was colonized by Indian races who brought their own cereals.

Amusements.—Cairo with its bright clear weather, lends itself so easily to an outdoor life that no one will be surprised to hear that the English colony has introduced some British sports. If we cross the Nile by its iron bridge, we at once come to a large park between the river and one of its branches. Here there are about fifty acres of grass belonging to the Ghezireh Sporting Club, and devoted to polo, cricket, football, golf, lawn-tennis, pigeon-shooting, etc. There is a course for riding and for leaping, and every winter there are two race meetings of two days each, three skye meetings, and six or seven Gymkhanas. Visitors may become temporary members of the club on paying £2. A regimental band plays most afternoons, and it is naturally the most favourite resort in Cairo. Our foreign friends sometimes play lawn-tennis, but usually confine themselves to looking on at the English. There are half a dozen lawn-tennis courts in the town, facilities for boxing and fencing, and excellent hacks for riding or driving all over the country.

The resources of the Nile have not yet been developed, and there is but little rowing, sailing, fishing, or swimming.

Shooting.—The visitor who wants big game will be disappointed in Egypt; but, on the other hand, he can get plenty of quail, duck, and snipe. He must bring an ordinary breech-loading gun with him, but all cartridges must be bought in Cairo, one maker having the exclusive monopoly. In 1889 an English visitor rode down and shot three wolves (*Canis variegatus*) beyond the Pyramids, but this is a unique experience. Ibex can be shot in the mountains near Suez; gazelle are very shy everywhere; wild pig can be got in the Fayoum and at Broullos, and lynx near Tel-el-Kebir; and in the desert there are jackal, hyena, fox, hare, and the long-eared Fennec fox. From October to March there is good snipe, duck, and geese shooting, and from February to May there is an abundance of quail. In February, 1889, two English visitors made a bag of forty duck and four hundred snipe in five days at Kafr-el-Sheikh, and this is only an instance of what many others have done. One hundred and twenty quail have been shot by two guns on the road to the Pyramids in March, between luncheon and dinner. Pigeon-shooting in the villages can be obtained all the year round, because pigeons are kept for the sake of their manure, and the natives are delighted at times to have some of the surplus birds killed. In January, 1889, two good shots brought down 282 pigeons within three hours at Beliana. Sandgrouse and plover can also be shot in the spring. No gun licence is necessary.

Sight-seeing.—There is a great deal to see in and near Cairo, enough to occupy a serious-minded individual for more than one winter, and fair accounts of most of the sights may be found in the guide-books. Besides the bazaars already mentioned, where the products not only of Egypt, but of Syria, Turkey, Persia, Tunis, and Asia Minor may be bargained for, the original walls and gates are well worth visiting. They date from the eleventh and twelfth centuries, and the old parts of the town, which are completely Oriental and highly picturesque, contain houses which have been built at all times during the last six hundred years. Many streets still exist where beautiful mushribyeh windows are numerous, and where minarets and mosques produce a view which is not seen in any other city. No greater change can be experienced in leaving these Coptic and Arab quarters than to find one's self in the European district where broad streets are laid out, and European houses and shops have been built since 1865.

A characteristic view of the town and the Pyramids plateau can be obtained from the citadel, especially at sunset, and leave should be sought to visit the English military hospital there, which is one of the finest in the world. The Turkish baths are not particularly clean or well cared for.

Mosques.—There are in Cairo some three hundred mosques, many of which are worth visiting. The following is a list of those which show best the wonderful art of the Saracens. They are placed in chronological order, and date from A.D. 640 to A.D. 1503. Amr, Ibn Tulun, Azhar, El Hakim, El Shafiy (mausoleum), Kalaun, El Maridany, Aksunkur (blue-tiled), Sultan Hassan, Barkuk, El Muayyad, Kait Bey, El Ghory (two). No visitor should miss seeing the Khedivial Library, which contains an unrivalled collection of Korans, Commentaries on the Koran, and Traditions, many of which have been taken for safe keeping out of the mosques above mentioned. Then, too, there is the Museum of Arab art, where are lamps of brass and of glass, chandeliers, tables, old mosque doors inlaid with ivory, and many other beautiful treasures, snatched a few years ago from the interior of uncared-for mosques.

Coptic churches.—These are deeply interesting, because the old buildings are in good preservation, and in their construction and fittings give us as accurate a picture of early Christian worship as can anywhere be found. Some of them still have convents adjoining, and are surrounded by thick walls like a fortress, telling tales of old persecution about the days of the fifth century, when the Bible was translated into the Coptic tongue.

Besides some of the usually visited churches in old Cairo, a Copt should be engaged to take the visitor to the Church of the Virgin, near the Mouski, where may be seen the original type of the Coptic basilica, with a *baldacchino* supported by four columns and semicircular stone seats arranged round the apse, and indeed much else of interest.

The modern Coptic cathedral is only worth visiting to see the service, such as on Easter Eve or Easter Day; but it must be remembered that their festivals sometimes take place according to our calendar, and sometimes by the Old Style, twelve days later.

A riding or driving excursion will of course be made to the necropolis of Kait Bey, and to the so-called tombs of the Memlooks.

The palaces of Shoobra, Ghezireh, and Ghizeh are all worth visiting if a permit can be obtained, because they have lovely gardens, and remind one of the former glories of late Khedives. It is to the last of these three that the Boulak Museum is now being transferred.

Visitors interested in Oriental education will like to see the Polytechnic School, that of the Arts and Sciences, a charity for the deaf, dumb, and blind, and the useful work started by the late Miss Whately.

The ordinary visitor demands at once to be taken to see the howling and dancing dervishes, and there are many other more interesting sects whose monasteries he may visit if he will. Perhaps one may be forgiven for reminding him that their fantastic worship plays to the Mussulman religion a part something analogous to the Salvation Army section of the Protestant Church.

But whether the traveller comes for days, weeks, or months, let us impress upon him the absolute duty of visiting Boulak Museum, and of not neglecting his chance of seeing monuments as old as the Pyramids, wooden statues of much the same date, a unique assembly of royal mummies and portraits painted years before the Old Masters. The great objection to the museum is that most of the objects are not labelled, and that the catalogue is atrociously bad. We may see there the jewellery worn by an Egyptian queen three thousand six hundred years ago, a trilingual inscription not unlike the "Rosetta stone," and tables of kings like the famous slab from Abydos. The museum is better than any in Europe, and is rich especially in monuments of the earliest Dynasties.

Cairo. 71

Festivals.—There are several old Egyptian and Coptic holidays which have the advantage of being on fixed dates, and can therefore be easily seen by reference to guide-books. But the purely Mussulman functions take place according to the Mohammedan calendar, the year of which is $11\frac{1}{4}$ days less than our own. The following dates are an approximate guess at the principal feasts; but it must be remembered that the actual date is often changed either as a matter of convenience, or to cause the chief holiday to fall upon the eve of Friday—

		1890.	1891.
Moolid of Rifáce	about	Feb. 6	Jan. 29
Moolid of Seyyideh Zeynab	,,	March 5	Feb. 25
Night of the Ascension	,,	March 16	March 5
Night of Half Shaaban	,,	April 3	March 23
Ramadan begins	,,	April 19	April 8
Night of Power	,,	May 14	May 3
Little Bairam	,,	May 19	May 8
Procession of Kisweh	,,	May 25	May 14
Start of the Mahmal	,,	June 10	May 30
Bairam feast	,,	June 26	June 15
Martyrdom of Hussein	,,	Aug. 25	Aug. 14
Return of the Mahmal	,,	Sept. 20	Sept. 9
Birthday of Mahomed	,,	Sept. 25–Oct. 2	Sept. 19-26
Birthday of Hassan and Hussein	,,	Dec. 9	Dec. 3

CHAPTER V.

Excursions from Cairo.

I have already said that the favourite ride or drive is in the direction of Ghezireh, where on Fridays and Sundays there is always a crush of carriages; but those who love peace will be happier on the roads leading to the Pyramids, or Heliopolis, or Shoobra, all soft, good roads, well shaded by the sycamore-fig or other trees.

Desert.—For visitors who can ride a great treat is in store. The desert can be reached on all sides most easily, and supplies a capital galloping ground and invigorating air which seems to put fresh life into both horse and rider. The popular idea in England is that a desert is always one vast plain of dazzling sand without undulations and without signs of life, and that at every step the luckless traveller must sink ankle-deep in tiring sand. The reality is a series of hills and valleys with innumerable changes of colour, and of lights and shades, and a crisp, firm ground upon which we can walk for miles without getting tired. Moreover, our desert is by no means a perfect desert like the Sahara, devoid of vegetation.

In February, after the winter rain, green herbs and bushes sprout in the hollows, ravines, and valleys, and the flora are at their finest in March and April. After this the sun becomes too hot for them, and in the summer only the deeper-rooted trees and shrubs remain. The desert thorn is beloved by camels; the zygophyllums are very common and always succulent, but they are too salt except for the hungriest camels. The bitter colocynth and senna are used by the Bedouins. The desert flora are by no means rich, but a hundred species can be collected by diligent amateurs, and the number of possible species is six hundred. Desert plants cannot be cultivated in gardens; but, on the other hand, those species that have found their way from civilized spots into the wilds, seem to thrive untended in the desert. Rabbits, hares, foxes, jerboas, and lizards, all desert-coloured like the camel, are the animals one meets with most often. In the neighbourhood of any old necropolis, we find bits of granite and other monuments which have now disappeared; relics of the flint age may be found by careful searching, and many geological remains, including numerous fragments of petrified wood.

It is a favourite donkey-ride towards the so-called petrified forest, and on the way one passes the Red Hill, which is composed of a very hard Miocene conglomerate of sand, pebbles, and fossil wood. The two Colossi at Thebes were made of this stone, and it is now used for macadamizing roads, and for making millstones.

Mineral springs.—About half an hour south of Cairo there is a spring in the desert, called *Ain-el-Syra*. There is a dark greenish basin some fifty yards square, surrounded by limestone formations, and with a thick deposit of black sulphur mud. It has a great reputation among the natives for skin-eruptions and especially for scabies, and its votaries also drink from the sulphur spring which feeds the basin, and which rids them of dyspepsia and constipation. The temperature of the water is 104° Fahr. beneath the surface, and 64·4° at the surface on a winter day. Specific gravity 1·092.

ANALYSIS OF ONE LITRE.

Chloride of sodium	59,640 grammes.
Sulphate of magnesium	34,280 ,,
Chloride of magnesium	18,600 ,,
Sulphate of lime	6,000 ,,
Chloride of calcium	1,400 ,,
Carbonate of lime	0,040 ,,
Bicarbonate of iron	0,040 ,,
	120,000

GAS.

Carbonic acid	·048 ,,

Abu-el-Saoud is another water named after an Egyptian doctor of the fifteenth century. It is without colour and odour, and keeps well in a hot country. It is in great request among some Europeans and natives for disorders of digestion, and it has a distinct aperient effect. Its source is said to be from the Mokattam hills, and it is drunk at an establishment in Old Cairo, or bottled there for home use. There is also a swimming bath there of temperature 86° Fahr. No accurate analysis has yet been made. Reaction neutral; no gas; temperature, 86° Fahr. The principal ingredients are sulphates of soda and magnesia, and chlorides of sodium, magnesium, and calcium. There are no nitrates or ammonia.

The Barrage should certainly be visited, if it is only to see how the pluck and skill of English engineers have made it possible for some nine feet of water to be held up at the times when every drop of the Nile is wanted for land-irrigation. It is a long ride, but a very pleasant trip by steamer or by train, and the neighbourhood is very pretty.

Sakkárah.—The pleasantest way of making this excursion is by steamer to and from Cairo; but even then there is a two hours' donkey-ride from the landing-place to the Necropolis. If a steamer cannot be obtained, it is quite possible to go by train; or delicate people who wish to minimize the fatigue may sleep at Helouan overnight, and cross the river next morning. Those who love riding can mount their ponies at Mena Hotel, and ride along the desert to Sakkárah, passing the Pyramids of Abooseer and the remains of several miles of cemeteries. The day's excursion is a very delightful one, but it is very tiring to those unaccustomed to donkey-riding. Early in the winter the scenery is quite lovely—the inundation covering the fields, and the peasants swarming up the lofty date palms to gather the fruit which grows so well on the site of Memphis. In the spring the waters have subsided again, and the mounds and pottery which represent the old city, can be better seen.

A huge fallen statue of Rameses II. was raised out of a pond by a few English subscribers in 1887, and in working at it another colossus was discovered close by. It is not generally known that the Egyptian antiquities on Shepheard's balcony came from Sakkárah, and bear evidence of having been visited *in situ* by Greek tourists, who scribbled their names in the days long ago before the stones were buried in sand, and then once more discovered by Mariette. Boulak and many European museums have been largely enriched by the treasures of Sakkárah, which represents about four square miles of the necropolis of Memphis. The monumental wonders are sufficiently set forth in the guide-books; but some of them are kept purposely buried in the sand to prevent destruction. It is usually said that the mummied bulls from the Apis Mausoleum are all lost, but the writer accidentally found three of them in 1887 in the Historical Society's Museum in New York. They were probably stolen and bought when the Serapeum was discovered in 1861. The tomb of Tih, of the Fifth Dynasty, contains wall sculptures in such excellent preservation that it should be visited by all; and there is another tomb kept closed which is by no means inferior. From these life-like sculptures and others much has been learnt about the manners and customs of those who lived more than five thousand years ago.

Recent discoveries in Egypt.*—Full accounts of the late discoveries of Mr. Flinders Petrie, and of Mr. Naville for the Egyptian Exploration Fund, have been published in their special transactions, but not yet in the guide-books, so the remainder of this chapter will be devoted to recapitulating them for the benefit of travellers who desire to visit the spots which have been worked during the English occupation.

1. Commencing with Lower Egypt, we have

---

* Mr. Petrie has kindly supplied me with much valuable information for this purpose.

Pithon (Tel-el-Maskhuta), near the modern station called Rameses, between Zagazig and Ismailia. From here statues have been sent to Boulak and the British Museum, and there are still remains of the Nineteenth Dynasty, and of the store-chambers built by the Israelites.

2. Goshen (Saft-el-Hennah), near the railway stations of Zagazig and Abu Hamad. A large sculptured shrine of the Thirtieth Dynasty now in Boulak came from there, but to-day there is nothing of special interest on the site.

3. Tanis (San-el-Haggar), twenty miles from Fakus by boat or donkey, and therefore rather troublesome to reach. There is an enormous temple, with statues of different periods from Twelfth to Nineteenth Dynasties, and it is the finest place for the tourist to visit till he gets southward to Thebes. It was excavated by Mariette and finished by Mr. Petrie, and large numbers of papyri were sent from it to the British Museum.

4. Tel Bedowi and Nebesheh stand half-way from Fakus to Tanis, and have furnished many gifts to the British Museum. There are still the temple of Aahmes of the Twenty-sixth Dynasty, a large shrine of Uati, and tombs and cemetery.

5. Zagazig (Tel Basta, or the Pibeseth of the Old Testament). There are records dating from the Fourth to Thirtieth Dynasties, and from here

came the large statues of the Hyksos period, and columns were removed to Boulak, British Museum, and the United States. The rest of the temple is still standing.

6. Onias (Tel-el-Yahoudi), near the station of Shibeen-el-Kanater. There was a Twentieth Dynasty palace, now destroyed, and there are tombs of a Greco-Jewish colony, a large Roman camp, and walls of plastered guard-houses three feet high.

7. Daphne (Defneh or Tahpanhes of Old Testament), twelve miles from Salahieh station, or from Kantara on the Suez Canal. Here there are remains of the fort mentioned by Jeremiah, and a Greek camp around it; Twenty-sixth Dynasty, or 660–560 B.C. Large quantities of painted archaic Greek pottery now in the British Museum came from here.

8. Naucratis (Tel Gaief), five miles from Teh-el-Baroud station. Here we may still see the site of the Greek town and temples to Apollo, Aphrodite, Dioscuri, etc., and by searching, many small objects and painted pottery can be found, date 660 B.C. to 200 A.D. A great deal of archaic Greek pottery was taken from here to the British Museum. It will be remembered that the site of Naucratis was quite lost, until one day Mr. Petrie was shown by a Bedouin a piece of a Greek statue near Cairo,

and, following up this clue, he discovered this interesting buried city.

9. But it is not only in the Delta that much has been brought to light. If the visitor will take the train southwards to Medineh-el-Fayoum, and entrust himself to a Greek inn lately opened there, he will find the site of a large temple at the north end of the town, and parts of a pylon still standing. Date from the Twelfth Dynasty to the time of Ptolemy II.

10. Biahmu is six miles north of Medineh-el-Fayoum, and here are the pedestals of the colossi of Amen-emhat III., who made Lake Mœris and the famous Labyrinth in the Twelfth Dynasty. The fragments found here are now at Oxford.

11. Howara is four miles east of Medineh-el-Fayoum. The Pyramid was tunnelled unsuccessfully from the north in 1888, and the true passage was opened from the south in 1889. Date, Amenemhat III. and his daughter Ptah-nefru of the Twelfth Dynasty. Her altar and her bowls are now at Boulak, as also the finest set of amulets known. The site of the Labyrinth is south of the Pyramid, where fragments of it can be seen. To the north of the Pyramid is the cemetery from which the Roman portraits were sent to Boulak, and to the National Gallery in London.

12. Illahun is thirteen miles east of Medineh-

el-Fayoum, and fourteen miles from Beni-souef station. Mr. Petrie has now opened this Pyramid also, and has cleared its temple, which is half a mile to the east. Fragments of this temple are now in England, dating from Usertasen II. of the Twelfth Dynasty. One of the most interesting discoveries is that the town of the builders of this Pyramid joins the temple on the north, and here may be seen rows of houses for workmen and for stores, and numerous flint instruments lying about. Many papyri and tools were found, and pottery with Cypriote letters on it, thus proving the early date of the Cypriote alphabet. There is plenty of pottery of the Twelfth Dynasty lying about; and to the west and south of the Pyramid is a cemetery which was originally used by the Twelfth Dynasty, and later used again from the Twenty-first to the Twenty-sixth. Near the temple are Coptic graves of the fourth century of the Christian era.

13. Medineh Grob (*i.e.* raven) is at the south end of the Illahun dyke, which originally dated from the Twelfth Dynasty, but has since shifted its position. Here there is a town of the Nineteenth Dynasty, built over the ruins of a temple of Thothmes III., and from here much Greek pottery of the Mycenæ type, with Cypriote and Phœnician letters on it, has been sent to the British Museum.

G

Behind the town is a cemetery, the south end of which contains graves of the Eighteenth to the Twentieth Dynasties, while the north was used during the Ptolemaic period. Many Greek and demotic papyri were found with the cartonnages of the mummies, and Boulak is now the proud possessor of two large bronze pans and three wooden statuettes of the Nineteenth Dynasty.

It is to be regretted that, while so much has been done by English enterprise, Boulak should have so few results to show from its own excavations. Many of the antiquities found pass into the hands of dealers; and so lately as 1888 several statues of great value of the Fourth and Fifth Dynasties were found at Memphis, and had afterwards to be bought by the Boulak Museum.

14. The cuneiform inscriptions of Tel-el-Amarna, the necropolis of part of the Eighteenth Dynasty, half-way between Cairo and Thebes, have lately been deciphered by Professor Sayce. From his unique researches we find that, one hundred years before the Exodus, active literary intercourse was going on between Babylon, Egypt, Palestine, and Syria, and this was carried on by means of the Babylonian cuneiform writing. He believes that Babylonian was as much the language of diplomacy and of cultivated society as French has been in modern times, though it must have taken years

of patient labour to read it. These tablets, so recently brought to light, give ground for supposing that there may be rich libraries buried in Syria and Palestine of clay tables inscribed in cuneiform characters.

CHAPTER VI.

SUBURBS OF CAIRO—HELOUAN-LES-BAINS—
PYRAMIDS—MATARIYEH.

HELOUAN is an artificial oasis in the desert, three miles from the right bank of the Nile, and fifteen miles south of Cairo. The railway connecting it with the capital has in 1889 been brought into the centre of the town, and various other improvements have been made by the company to whom the railway now belongs. The trains run to and fro in forty minutes, and six times a day. The village consists of a palace built by the present Khedive, two hotels, about a hundred and fifty detached private houses, and two engines for pumping up Nile water. It is about 112 feet above the Nile level, on a firm plateau of sand, and is famous for a remarkably pure, dry, and dustless atmosphere. It is surrounded on all sides by the desert, and on the east by the continuation of the Mokattam range of hills. But the property which makes the table-land of Helouan remarkable is that it is in some places saturated with water like a sponge. Water is found at a depth varying from ten inches to ten feet, and, when coming out of the springs, has a temperature of 77° or 85° Fahr., and the yield from these springs is considerable. The water of the sulphur springs is quite clear and colourless, but, on being exposed for a short time to the air, the surface becomes covered with a slight film of sulphur and lime-salts. The water smells a little of sulphuretted hydrogen, and is slightly saltish without being unpleasant to drink. Up to the present twelve springs have been discovered, and may be divided into three classes—Sulphur, Iron, and Saline.

1. Two of the Sulphur springs supply the Baths which are attached to the chief hotel, and a third has been led into a fountain, where the poor of the neighbourhood come to drink gratis. Temperature, 86° Fahr.; specific gravity, 1·0025.

GASTINEL BEY'S ANALYSIS OF ONE LITRE (35 FLUID OZ.).

Chloride of sodium	3·2000 grammes.
Chloride of magnesium	1·8105 ,,
Bicarbonate of lime	·8050 ,,
Sulphate of lime	·2100 ,,
Chloride of calcium	·1880 ,,
Silica	·0150 ,,
Organic matter	·0015 ,,
	6·2300 ,,

GAS.

Sulphuretted hydrogen	47 c.c.	·0731 grammes.
Carbonic acid	61 ,,	·1200 ,,
Nitrogen	10 ,,	·0126 ,,
	118	·2057

There are two other sulphur springs, less warm and containing much more salt, but they are not being used at present. The sulphur waters resemble those of Aix-les-Bains and Enghien (Paris).

2. There are two Iron springs, the water of which is pleasant to drink and is taken gratis by large numbers of people. The bicarbonate of iron in the water comes from the protoxide of iron in the sand. The sand, which in the spring is black, takes a yellowish-grey colour when dried in the air, the protoxide being turned into sesquioxide of iron. The water is clear, colourless, odourless, and tastes a little salt and bitter. Temperature, 77° Fahr.; specific gravity, 1·0445. It does not leave a deposit of carbonate of iron when exposed to the air.

ANALYSIS OF ONE LITRE.

Chloride of sodium	37·2671 grammes.
Chloride of magnesium	10·6020 ,,
Bicarbonate of lime	5·9422 ,,
Sulphate of magnesium	2·3507 ,,
Chloride of calcium	1·5250 ,,
Sulphate of lime	1·0820 ,,

Sulphate of alumina	·5861	grammes.
Bicarbonate of soda	·2255	,,
Bicarbonate of iron	·0555	,,
Organic matter	·0300	,,
Silica	·0180	,,
	59·6841	,,

GAS.

Carbonic acid	26 c.c.	·0511	grammes.

Lovers of this water take it for its aperient rather than its ferruginous effect.

3. There is only one Saline spring; the water acts as a purgative, and is bottled to be drunk at leisure by its devotees. The water, like the others, is clear, colourless, and without odour, and has a slight salt, bitter taste. Temperature, 77° Fahr.; specific gravity, 1·0152.

ANALYSIS OF ONE LITRE.

Chloride of sodium	4·0171	grammes.
Chloride of magnesium...	3·1158	,,
Bicarbonate of lime	1·2569	,,
Sulphate of magnesia	1·0798	,,
Sulphate of soda	·4468	,,
Sulphate of alumina	·4257	,,
Chloride of calcium	·1610	,,
Organic matter	·0330	,,
Sulphate of lime	·0210	,,
Silica	·0100	,,
	10·5671	,,

GAS.

Carbonic acid ...	6 c.c.	·01179	grammes.

But, though I give an analysis of all three kinds of waters, the only important one at present is the sulphur variety. It owes its sulphur properties to the chemical processes which sulphate of lime, meeting with nitrogenous matter and becoming sulphate of calcium, produces by setting free carbonic acid and nitrogen from the decomposition of the nitrogenous matter. Then the carbonic acid decomposes the sulphate of calcium and forms carbonate of lime, which, in presence of an excess of carbonic acid and under great pressure, is converted into a very soluble bicarbonate of lime, which at last sets free sulphuretted hydrogen gas. The nitrogenous organic matter which is found in all the Helouan waters has been named Barégine, because it was first discovered in the Baróges waters of the Pyrenees. It is found in all sulphur waters when exposed to light and air, and is the cause of the greenish vegetation which collects round the edges of stagnant sulphur water. The sulphur is sufficiently strong in the air to turn silver ornaments black, but after the first day one ceases to notice the odour.

History.—The village is said to take its name from the great grandson of a certain untraceable king of Egypt. It is known to have been frequented in A.D. 690, and at other times by notables who were driven out of Old Cairo by the plague, but various fires have destroyed all trace of former dwellings. There remain, however, for those who dig, the *débris* of bricks, granite, marble, pottery, glass, and even coins.

After the records of Arab historians we come down to 1830, when Linant Pasha, a French engineer, discovered that the region of sulphur springs extended southward from Helouan to opposite Benisuef, where borings used to be made by the natives, who bathed in the springs and built tents near them. In 1849 the Egyptian Government took possession of Helouan, built wooden huts, and even sent sick soldiers to be experimented on by the waters. The results were so satisfactory that the spot began to be a little popular, but it was not until 1871 that the Government could make up its mind either to work the springs itself or to let them to an intelligent European. In that year a Dr. Reil was appointed Director of the Baths, a small town began gradually to spring up, and in 1873 the Grand Hotel was built and was confided to its present manager. Trees were planted, the swamps were drained, and in 1876 a railway from Cairo was opened. Great improvements have been made to the baths, and the place is every year becoming more popular, the number of baths during 1885 having been only 7031, and being now doubled every year.

Baths.—In an establishment where crowned heads are visitors, and which humbly imitates the huge establishments in Europe, it is needless to say that no cost has been spared in putting the bath-houses into excellent order. Special arrangements are made for ladies, both natives and Europeans. The corridors are paved with marble, and fifteen bath-rooms and the actual baths are made of enamelled porcelain tiles. Electric bells, good furniture, ventilation, thermometer, sand-glass, etc., are provided. There are shower-baths and ordinary hot-water baths for those who do not wish to undergo any cure, and delightful swimming-baths for the two sexes. The bath-rooms are kept beautifully clean, and the ascent and descent is made easy for those who are too crippled to walk. An inhalation-room is provided for the asthmatics who wish to inhale sulphuretted gas straight from one of the springs.

The water that has been used in the baths is run off into the desert two miles away by cemented covered drains, and these have also been utilized for draining the marshy parts of the desert land. The result has been that malaria has disappeared, the air is drier, and the spot as a health-resort is rapidly increasing in popularity. An Austrian medical man lives in the chief hotel, and has made a speciality of electricity and electric baths.

A druggist is provided by the Government, but many European visitors prefer to be dependent upon Cairo for their doctors and drugs.

There are two hotels, the larger of which is in connection with the baths, and has forty-six bedrooms, some of which are very large, also a lawn-tennis court. There is easy telephone and telegraph communication with Cairo.

Furnished and unfurnished villas can be hired near the Bath Establishment.

Course of baths.—The water for the baths has a temperature of about 86° Fahr. upon coming out of the spring, and this can be artificially heated to 102°, or more, in pipes which prevent any evaporation of gas. But it is doubtful whether it is ever necessary to take the bath above 100°, for hotter baths are generally apt to exhaust the patient. The baths are open from 6 a.m. to 8 p.m., and may be taken as it suits the convenience of the patient—say one hour before meals, or three or four hours after meals. There can be no object in taking more than one bath in the day, though robust men who are in a hurry to get through their course can easily stand an occasional second bath in the twenty-four hours. The beginner should not stay in the water longer than fifteen minutes, but he may gradually increase this to thirty minutes. If he is not under medical supervision the whole time, he should invariably report progress to his doctor during the third week of the cure, as a tonic is then often necessary, and he may be unconsciously overdoing the treatment.

Delicate people should begin with a temperature not above 98°, should take a bath on alternate days, and not for more than ten minutes at a time.

It is hardly necessary to remind patients whose hearts are affected that they should have medical advice upon the desirability of hot bathing. The Helouan waters, as I have already said, are stronger than those of Aix-les-Bains, but they have not yet the advantage of being accompanied by all the excellent system of douches and local massage for which the Savoy resort is so famous.

Invalids are often chary of transporting themselves and their relatives from the gaieties of Cairo to the solitude of Helouan, and to them it can only be said that, if their physical strength permits, they are easily able to live in Cairo, and to go four or five days a week to Helouan to take their baths. But though some men and a few women prefer to do this, there can be no doubt that the purer air, earlier hours, and complete repose of the desert life are most useful adjuncts to the sulphur baths—and such invalids occasionally need reminding that they have come abroad for their health, and not for the distractions of their friends.

Suburbs of Cairo. 93

When the course of baths is completed, a bracing change is not necessary; but if it has taken place in the spring, the sea-voyage to Europe seems always beneficial.

The sulphur-water may be used not only in the form of baths, but locally, as by fomentations, gargles, or injections. When swallowed, its action has hardly yet been determined, but it is apparently quite harmless. The great value of Helouan is, of course, in relation to the treatment of rheumatic diseases, and such a sanatorium during the winter months is a boon to every prescribing physician in inclement England. It is quite open to those who desire to take their fill of sulphur baths to spend the winter in Cairo and at Luxor, and take a course of baths at Helouan at any time between November and April, and then to proceed to Aix-les-Bains, where the best time for a course is from May 10 to June 10, as advised by Sir A. Garrod and others. By skilful management, the rheumatic patient can ensure remaining both at Helouan and afterwards at Aix in a temperature which is very like London in the warm days of July.

The number of baths at Helouan is a very important question. During the first week the patient feels no result; during the second, his rheumatic pains are a little increased; and during the third, he feels great benefit from the baths, though this benefit is likely to be increased still further after he leaves the place. As the end of the third week approaches he feels a little lassitude and fatigue, and requires to be watched by a careful eye. The number of baths varies from eighteen or nineteen in delicate women who cannot stand further heat, to twenty-four in robust patients.

It is specially in the treatment of *rheumatoid arthritis* that Helouan is most successful, improving the patient's state at the time, and rendering him less liable to acute attacks in the future, the improvements, as I have just said, often going on in his system for six months.

As at all other similar establishments, there is a favourable record of individual cripples who are laboriously carried to the springs, and eventually walk away wreathed in joy!

Helouan is not yet widely known to the medical profession or to the public; but the cases of this disease which have given the bath a fair trial have invariably improved.

Helouan is of no avail for cases of acute or recent *gout*, and might even do harm by checking the local manifestation of a constitutional poison. In chronic gouty swelling or stiffness, or gouty tendency, eczema, psoriasis, or in that form of gout which is not connected with portal congestion, the cure is of use, because the skin and kidneys are made to act better, and the interval between acute attacks may be prolonged.

Again, in sub-acute *rheumatism*, or in cases with recent cardiac mischief, the baths are not indicated; but in all cases of chronic rheumatism, whether of joints, muscles, or nerve-sheaths, great benefit is always derived. Some troublesome cases of sciatica, too, have got great good from Helouan, and all local affections dependent on rheumatism and gout, or connected with either of them, have a good chance of being either cured or relieved.

As might be expected, some diseases of the skin, such as eczema, acne, prurigo, ecthyma, scabies, etc., get great benefit here, and it is believed that the waters would prove of value in leprosy if a separate establishment could be specially built for the few natives afflicted with it. The baths have been strongly recommended for inveterate cases of syphilis, dysmenorrhœa, amenorrhœa, endocervicitis, leucorrhœa, some cases of sterility, cystitis, and even diabetes. The inhalation and gargles are said to be of use for bronchitis, asthma, and laryngeal, pharyngeal, and nasal catarrh. Good has often resulted from the employment of baths in cases of old gunshot wounds, or in the stiffness resulting from fractures or sprains. I advised a patient once to try the baths for incipient locomotor ataxy, but he found no benefit from them, and believed that the hot water was distinctly injurious to him.

Excursions.—On all sides there is the desert for walking or donkey-riding, and there are two roads for carriage-exercise. Near the hills flint implements can be found. There are some old alabaster quarries to visit, and in the same neighbourhood is an old dam discovered by Professor Schweinfurth.

Shooting-parties sometimes go out for gazelles, hyenas, wolves, foxes, and jackals.

I have already said that the trip to Sakkárah can very conveniently be made from Helouan, and one can also go to the quarries of Toura and Maaserah, which are of great extent and wonderfully interesting. From them came the stone blocks and casing of the Ghizeh Pyramids, and as the quarries are still used to supply flagstones, we can compare the rough work of the present masons with the dexterous neatness of past ages. No cartouches have been discovered in the quarries older than the Twelfth Dynasty, and perhaps the commonest seen to-day is that of Hakor of the Twenty-ninth.

An intelligent donkey-boy will help us to explore one of the many waterless valleys of the neighbourhood, where the dry water-courses still have green tufts on the banks, and we find *sycophyllum*, belladonna, and heather growing, while, if it chances to be February or May, we are in luck, and see many desert flowers. We can trace the former ravages of the Mediterranean Sea; we find stray pieces of petrified wood, coprolites, and fossilized oyster-beds. The only live things we see are vultures, rabbits, martens, chameleons, lizards, locusts, and innumerable snails, till we come upon a gipsy Bedouin, with one cotton rag tied over his head and crossed round his neck, and a second tied round his waist. He has a lean donkey or two feeding on the stray tufts, a long pipe, a powder-horn, some shot, and a drink of water, which he willingly gives us. In the mountains, we stumble on a dry waterfall with a sheer precipice of several hundred feet, and boulders rounded by torrential waters; and though we walk and explore nearly the whole day, we suffer very little fatigue, because the cool breeze of the desert is as invigorating as a sparkling wine.

The Pyramids.

Twenty-two years ago, visitors to the Pyramids at Ghizeh were obliged to rise very early in the morning, mount donkeys to the river's edge, whence they were ferried across, and had to be dependent again on donkeys for a long *détour* by the banks of winding canals, till at last they reached the desert, hastily visited the Pyramids, and then had to return at once to reach Cairo before sunset. Those who desired to devote a longer time to the sights took out with them tents, a cook, food, and a guard of Bedouins.

Now matters are all changed; the tourist drives from his hotel to the Great Pyramid in a little more than an hour, and commonly makes the trip between luncheon and dinner. There is a good made road all the way, lined with trees, and flanked on both sides either by the huge irrigation basins during the autumn inundation, or by miles of green cultivated land, in which buffaloes, children, and camels are dotted about.

Mena Hotel.—Those who do not know the Cairo of to-day will be most surprised at the existence of a first-class hotel at the foot of the Pyramids, and just seven miles from the heart of the town. Its history is this: In 1884, an Englishman, suffering from chronic phthisis, bought from the Government a desert property of three hundred acres, including a house, in which he and his wife lived very comfortably. He believed that the air was more beneficial to him than that of the other health-resorts he had tried, and though he had had a moribund appearance for two years, he certainly improved markedly in health and strength. He remained there two winters and a summer, and was progressing well until he was persuaded, during the second summer, to try a change to the mountain air of Cyprus, where he very soon died. Before his death he had commenced to build a sanatorium, to give others the opportunity of living in a climate which had apparently been so beneficial to himself.

The property was then bought by an English resident of Cairo, who determined to open an hotel, and, while providing visitors with all necessary luxuries, to prevent the neighbourhood of the Pyramids from being spoilt by incongruous behaviour. The hotel at once became popular, in consequence of the extreme purity of the air, the delicious repose of the desert, the convenient proximity to Cairo, and the unrivalled interest of the locality. Twice its owner has had to treble its size, and now it contains eighty bedrooms, a dining-room 40 × 80 ft., another 40 × 27 ft., smaller dining-rooms, drawing and reading-rooms, full-sized English billiard-tables, an ice-room, studio for artists, etc. There is a Jenning's lavatory, and the earth-closets are in a building disconnected from the hotel. There are six fixed baths, hot and cold, and the bath and sink water is used to irrigate the garden; also a swimming-bath, 80 × 25 ft. The drinking-water is obtained from wells in the desert, fifty feet deep, and is conducted through filtering-tanks to the hotel. An English medical man is resident during the season, and his colleagues in Cairo can also be summoned by telephone or donkey-messenger. Among other things provided for the comfort of English visitors are a steam-laundry, smoking-rooms, magazines and news-papers, and stabling for thirty-two horses. For amusements there are an archery ground and lawn-tennis court, golf-links, and the makings of a polo and cricket ground. There are ponies, camels, and donkeys to ride, traps to hire, and good quail and duck-shooting. A four-in-hand coach is to drive daily from Cairo during the season, November to April. Price 12s. to 14s. a day, with no extras.

During the last two winters I have sent many patients to stay at this hotel, and have been much pleased with their progress. It is also very useful for those in Cairo who wish to drive out for luncheon or afternoon tea in the winter, or for dinner upon moonlit nights in the warmer weather. The air is so pure and dry that it cannot be praised too highly, but it must be remembered that of the three desert spots recommended near Cairo, none are so warm as Luxor; but, on the other hand, they are invaluable to those who do not want the fatigue and expense of a voyage up the Nile. The temperature of all three resorts, Helouan, Pyramids, and Matariyeh, may be taken as the same as that given for Cairo, with the difference of a little less humidity in their favour. As in Cairo, there is a great fall in temperature soon after the sun has set, and invalids must either be indoors or provided with wraps, but fortunately there is no danger of malaria.

Sight-seeing.—About forty years ago, when Lepsius visited the Pyramids, and had his encampment partly washed away by a fierce rain-storm, there were no less than sixty-five Pyramids on the plateau of Ghizeh; but now there are only nine recognized, and of these visitors pay homage to the three largest. I have so often been summoned to attend patients with weak hearts who have suffered after rapidly ascending the Great Pyramid, that I am constrained to warn all those who are elderly and delicate from attempting it. The climb is a difficult one of at least twenty or thirty minutes, and the only satisfaction to be gained is a beautiful view from the summit. The staff on the top of this Pyramid dates from the transit of Venus expedition of 1874.

There are always Bedouins who will be delighted for a small sum to ascend one or both Pyramids in an incredibly short time, and a patient of mine with a weak heart was induced last winter after dinner to imitate the performance. He won his wager, and also a week's fright and rest in bed. The descent from the Pyramid is more unpleasant to most people than the being hauled up.

The visit to the interior is quite worth the fatigue to those who are fairly strong, because the traveller then gets an accurate idea of what these gigantic tombs were intended for.

The best way to avoid all altercation with the Bedouins, who are pleasant, amiable, and gentlemanly, with an eye fixed on the main chance, is to let them choose one of their number to take charge of the party, and to receive all the backsheesh. It will then be to his interest to protect the party from all his brethren; and it may be said generally that if any difficulty arises it is the fault of the traveller.

The road up the Pyramid hill was repaired in 1881 from chips of the casing of the Great Pyramid; and, in addition to many other thefts during several ages, the Sultan Hassam mosque is said to have been built in A.D. 1056, from the stones of the Great Pyramid. It seems to have been less trouble for Cairo architects to take their stone from Memphis and the Pyramids than to have it hewn afresh from the quarries which originally supplied it, and were actually nearer to Cairo.

The Pyramid-builders were masters of the art

of cementing. In the Great Pyramid there are 2,300,000 stones, and blocks weighing about sixteen tons have vertical joints only one-fiftieth of an inch thick in the casing. Fancy this for thirteen acres of surface, and there are tens of thousands of casing stones, none less than one ton in weight!

The granite Temple is connected with the Second Pyramid by a causeway, and, to rightly understand the Pyramids, it should be remembered that each one had a temple on its east where the dead and deified king was worshipped, just as humbler folk worshipped their ancestors in their family tombs.

The guide-books tell of most of the tombs to be seen here, but visitors often neglect to see the galleries of the workmen, which are rather interesting. There are altogether ninety-one galleries, 9½ ft. wide, and 7 ft. high, with an aggregate of 1½ mile of length.

The Sphinx, as the largest and perhaps the oldest sculptured figure in the world, is fascinating to all; but those who wish to worship unrestrainedly, must go there with a carefully chosen party by moonlight. Perhaps the best view of it is obtained from the steps facing it, which is probably the spot chosen by the original worshippers of the god. As visitors sometimes forget the sex of the sphinx, I may remind them that his beard, broken in pieces, is now in the British Museum.

Near the Third Pyramid there are the ruins of a Græco-Roman village.

Besides the ride to Sakkárah, excursions may be made to the Pyramid of Abu Roash, or to a petrified forest seven miles away.

MATARIYEH.

Five miles to the north-east of Cairo, and now connected with it by train and telephone, is the village of Matariyeh, which has lately become a popular suburb among some of the European and native residents.

On Easter Monday, 1889, which is a national holiday in Egypt, 19,000 people were conveyed to it by train. At other times it is dull and empty, though two small hotels have lately sprung up, besides restaurants and many private villas. There is some talk of building an English hotel near the plain where, in A.D. 1517, the battle of Heliopolis made the Turks masters of Egypt, and where Kleber regained Cairo for a short time in 1800. The attractions offered to the guests would be camel-riding in the desert to Abbassiyeh, which was a suburb built in 1849 to please the Bedouin sheiks who declined to enter the city of Abbas, the then Khedive, or to the ostrich-farm and orange-groves in the neighbourhood. Then there are the petrified forest; the Virgin's Tree, which was planted in 1672; the oldest Obelisk in Egypt, and the mounds which represent Heliopolis, the celebrated town where Joseph married the high priest's daughter, where Moses became learned in the wisdom of the Egyptians, where Jeremiah wrote his Lamentations, and where Plato pondered over the new doctrine of the immortality of the soul.

CHAPTER VII.

Voyage up the Nile.

The traveller who wishes to visit Luxor, Thebes, Philæ, or Abu Simbel, is dependent upon the great water-way of Egypt. He may go up all the way by steamer or by dahabiyeh, or he may, if he chooses, save himself 230 miles by taking the train from Cairo to Assiout. In 1891, the Upper Egypt railway will have a station in Cairo itself, and will be pushed on to Girgeh, ninety-two miles south, so that patients will be able to leave Cairo one morning and sleep in Luxor the second night. But at present we are dependent on a railway station three miles outside Cairo, and a tiresome dusty journey of eleven hours is necessary to reach Assiout. Moreover, the invalid has the double disadvantage of starting from Cairo before the day is warmed by the sun, and of reaching Assiout after sunset. On the other hand, he has the advantage of getting without delay into the warmer latitude, and of escaping all risk of cold and draught on the river north of Assiout. Each individual case must be settled upon its own merits, and care taken to secure the minimum cold and fatigue.

There are many people who make the Nile trip without leaving their steamer or dahabiyeh, and some even make two steamer trips up the Nile in one winter. Cook's steamers are made as comfortable as possible, and he does everything he can to minimize the draught and cold for delicate passengers. His firm has what is almost a complete monopoly of the river traffic south of Cairo, and, as some 1500 visitors proceeded up the Nile in the winter of 1888–9, those intending to do so would be wise to secure accommodation in advance.

Four large steamers, luxuriously fitted up, ply between Cairo and Assouan between November and March, and on each of them there are two rooms nine or ten feet high specially reserved for invalids who are obliged to keep their cabins until they reach the universal sunshine of Luxor. The ordinary cabins have one or two berths, and convey fifty first-class passengers, and are provided with electric bells, and windows protected by glass, Venetians, and wire gauze. There are also ladies' saloons, piano, and library, and a plentiful supply of fresh food of all kinds.

Every steamer, large and small, carries an

English doctor, whose services are seldom required; a huge medicine-chest; a European manager; and a dragoman, who arranges the details of the sight-seeing.

The whole trip from Cairo to Assouan and back to Cairo in these steamers takes three weeks; or it may be arranged that the traveller shall break his journey for a long or short time at Luxor or elsewhere. For those who desire to visit all the temples and to devote a longer time to their study, a special steamer makes the trip in four weeks instead of three, and is provided with perfect accommodation for twenty-five passengers. The length of the smallest of these steamers is 160 ft.; the breadth, 20 ft.; the horse-power, 275; and the usual speed, eleven miles an hour.

But it has been found that there are many who cannot afford the time or the expense for the three weeks' trip, and therefore some cheap express steamers have been constructed to ply twice a week between Assiout and Assouan, so that tourists can go from Cairo to the First Cataract and back in fourteen days for £25, including a stay of four days at Luxor; or they may go to Luxor and back for £20 in eleven days, four of which can be devoted to seeing Thebes and Karnak. These cheaper steamers carry thirty first-class passengers, and are very useful for those invalids who wish to get quickly and inexpensively to the hotels at Luxor. Special facilities are made *en route* for postal and telegraphic communication with Cairo and with Europe.

Messrs. Cook are always able to provide families or shooting-parties with dahabiyehs and competent dragomans, or these may be engaged from many native owners.

The voyage up the Nile was formerly reserved for the richest English and Americans, but I have shown that it is now made easy for any one who wishes to spend £100 in pursuit of health or pleasure. There are many who are not sufficiently gregarious to wish to make a pleasure-trip with a number of strangers, and to see the sights at a fixed time and within a fixed period, and, moreover, have not to consider the economy of time or money. To them the peaceful life of a dahabiyeh has many attractions: their party is complete in itself; they have a supply of books, sketching-materials, shooting necessaries and patience; and a dragoman who will procure for them every day a fresh supply of milk, meat, vegetables, fruit, poultry, and eggs. They will be dependent on their cook for bread, and on various tins for butter, jam, bacon, biscuits, etc. They had better provide their own wine, curtains for draughty windows, and deck-chairs. They may either start in their dahabiyeh from Cairo, or send it up to Rodah or Assiout and there join it by train, or, best of all, engage a steamer to tow them at least as far as Assiout. This is a very delightful way of travelling, but the number of tow steamers is limited, and the price often prohibitive. The ordinary dahabiyeh, in going up stream against a current of three miles an hour, is quite dependent on wind. Fortunately the prevailing wind is from the north, the sails are large, and the crew are clever to take all advantage of it. It will take about two months to get to the First Cataract and back, and three months to go from Cairo to the Second Cataract and back, and the cost for a party of four is about twenty-five shillings per head per day.

There ought to be no mosquitoes on the Nile, or other biting insects, but flies are often a great trouble, and require whisks, papers, and traps. It is very cold at night, and ulsters, rugs, and other warm wraps are necessary.

Temperature and climate on the Nile in winter.— Dr. Patterson * gives an analysis for October, of six daily observations during a voyage from Cairo to Luxor and back. The thermometer varied from 68° at 7 a.m. to 82·5° at 3 p.m., the total mean of the month being 76° Fahr., and no rain fell during the time.

* "Egypt and the Nile," p. 20, 1867.

In November,* between Cairo and Assiout the deck temperature varies from $53°$ at 7 a.m. to $63°$ at noon and to $58°$ after sunset, which is also the mean of the month. The wind is north to northeast; there is a little dew at night, and a warmer coat is necessary on deck after sunset. The saloon temperature of November varies from $55°$ to $72°$, with an average of $66°$.

In December, Patterson gives as the result of two years' observations (1860-1-2) a minimum on deck of $47°$, a maximum of $68·5°$, and a mean of $57°$. The range is greater, so that once on December 29, the morning observation was $52°$, and at midday $72°$. The saloon temperatures of another observer give a minimum of $47°$; maximum, $79°$; and mean, $63°$; and his results of ninety-three psychrometrical readings give as average humidity in 1888, in the dahabiyeh saloon, 59 per cent., with a range from 43 to 78. The thermometer is highest at 3 p.m. and lowest between midnight and 7 a.m. The air is driest in the afternoon, and dampest in the early morning. Dr. F. S. Worthington has also given me some careful daily readings for December, 1888, between Cairo and a few miles to its south. The barometer average (corrected for sea-level) was 30·19; in the dahabiyeh saloon the average maximum temperature

* Average of three observers.

was 68°, and the minimum 52·3°; in the bed-room the figures were 66·5° and 57°; and the average minimum on deck was 43°. Nine days were cloudy and rather cold; the remainder were bright, fresh, and fine.

In January, Patterson gives the early morning temperature on deck as 50°; the maximum, 64·5°; and the mean, 56°. He notes that there was one shower of rain, and that the average daily range of the thermometer was from 4° to 7° Fahr. Dr. Worthington found that in January, 1889, between a point south of Cairo and another south of Girgheh, the barometer average was 30·17; the dahabiyeh saloon temperature showed a maximum of 69·6°, and a minimum of 50·7°, with a deck minimum of 41·5°. He recorded a south wind on sixteen days, north wind twelve days, rain on two days, and fog early in the morning on two other occasions, all the other days being bright and fine. Dr. T. D. Savill spent January, 1888, in one of Cook's steamers, travelling from Cairo to Wady Halfa and back, and kindly took some notes for me. His thermometers were hung below the awning where the passengers sit by day. He found the average maximum 70·3°, and the absolute maximum 77° (above Assouan); the average minimum 47·2°, and the absolute minimum 40° one night at Luxor. On eighteen different nights the temperature fell below 50°, and the average mean (mean of means) was 60°. He also occasionally tested the temperature an hour before and an hour after sunset; the average fall of six evenings was 3° Fahr. The usual wind was northerly, light to fresh. There were four days on which showers of rain fell, all south of Assouan; eight other days which were a little cloudy; and the remainder had perfect sunshine. The average humidity was 62 per cent., five times it was above 80, and the driest day it was only 34.

In February, Patterson gives a mean temperature of 63°, and a maximum of only 70°, with the record of one rain-shower, and an average range of the month from 4° to 5° Fahr. He speaks, however, of one strange day when the thermometer at 7 a.m. marked 44°, and rose at 2 p.m. to 76°, the solar temperature at that time being 135°, and at sunset the thermometer fell again 6° in half an hour. Dr. Worthington spent February, 1889, between Keneh and Assouan, and registered an average barometer of 30·23, an average maximum in the saloon of 76·3°, and minimum average 53·8°, while the minimum average on deck was 45·6°. The wind blew from the north twenty-one days, and from the south six days, there being twice clouds of dust in the air, but all the other days were bright and fine. In February, 1888, Dr.

I

Savill was travelling from Cairo to Wady Halfa, back again almost as far as Cairo, and then once more up the river to Luxor. His average maximum was 80·8°, and he reached his highest, 95°, one day above Luxor. His average minimum was 55·2°, and the lowest attained was 45°, there being five night-readings below 50°. The average mean of the month was 67·5°. The temperature as tested one hour before and one hour after sunset showed an average fall of 3·6° Fahr. The wind was northerly and light. On two days showers fell at Luxor, three other days were partially cloudy, but the remainder were sunny all day. The humidity ranged from 24 to 80, and the month's average was 49·5 per cent.

For March, Patterson's average is 66·3°, and his maximum only 71·5°, with the record of a thunderstorm two days in succession in one year. On two days of warm south winds he found the temperature differing 21° and 29° between 7 a.m. and midday, and the average range of the month a little higher than in February. The warmth of the Nile water taken at various times and places was 64°. Dr. Worthington drifted down the Nile from Assouan to Assiout in March, 1889, and recorded as barometer average, 30·21; as maximum saloon temperature, 82°; and as minimum average of saloon, 61·4°, and of deck, 55·5°. The wind was from the north twenty-two days, and from the south five days, and was entered as light every day excepting on nine occasions, when it was strong breeze or moderate gale. No rain was noted. During the first half of March, 1888, Dr. Savill accompanied a Cook's steamer from Luxor to Assouan and back again to Cairo by river, to bring back the last of the visitors from Luxor. The average maximum temperature under the awnings was 84°, and the highest point 100° was reached at Assouan. The average minimum was 51·7°, and the lowest recorded was 44°, there being four readings at night below 50°. The average mean was 67·8°. The temperature before and after sunset showed a fall of 4° Fahr. The wind was northerly and strong. There was no rain, one day was cloudy, the others sunny, and the humidity of the air very much less than in February.

April is not a month which many people spend on the river, on account of the increasing heat and the liability to dust-storms.

Dr. Worthington's observations were made during the former half of the month between Minieh and Cairo, and during the latter half on the same dahabiyeh at Cairo. The barometer remained at 30·15; the saloon maximum temperature averaged 81·7°, and the average minimum was 61° in the saloon and 53° on deck. The wind was northerly or north-west, and on eight days strong.

Dr. Worthington's records for May were still on the dahabiyeh at Cairo, during weather which most people found unpleasantly hot. His barometer average was 30·26; the maximum saloon average was 86·5°, and the average minimum heat was 67·6° in the saloon and 64·7° on deck. Wind was north-west, north-east, and north. There were three scorching hot days, and on the evening of the 23rd there was a little rain.

Places of interest.—The following sights can be easily visited during the voyage up the Nile: Sakkárah, Maydoum Pyramid, sugar-factories, grottoes of Beni Hassan, Tel-el-Amarna, Assiout, Ekhmeem where there has been a recent find of antiquities, Abydos, Denderah, Luxor, Karnak, Thebes, Esneh, Edfu, Silsileh, Komombo, Assouan, Elephantine Island, and Philæ.

There are many who wish to go higher than the First Cataract and to see the wonders of Kalabsheh, Abu Simbel, and Wady Halfa; but for this, special arrangements are necessary both by steamer and by dahabiyeh.

The chief monuments of the Nile are south of Assiout, so that no invalid who has seen Sakkárah while in Cairo need grudge the few remaining sights which he will miss by taking train to Assiout.

Birds of the Nile.—I have already said that there is excellent shooting during the winter months, but to enjoy this thoroughly the sportsman must be on a dahabiyeh, and not tied to time. There is a great variety of duck and small and large waders, and any number of grain-eating birds and insect-devourers. Ornithologists interested in collecting birds will find a larger range of hawk species up the Nile than in almost any other country. A complete list of birds is too long for insertion here, but a traveller going to Assouan at the beginning of the year is certain, among others, to meet with the following:—Griffon vulture and Egyptian vulture, imperial eagle, spotted eagle, rock pigeon, Egyptian turtle-dove, chiffchaff, white-winged chat, kestrel, lesser kestrel, scops owl, Egyptian eagle owl, Egyptian goose, common teal, parasitic kite, Oriental chimney swallow, pale crag swallow, Egyptian goatsucker, black and white kingfisher, common kingfisher, buff-backed heron, common heron, night heron, black-headed plover, grey-headed yellow wagtail, desert bullfinch, white-winged wagtail, spur-winged plover, common quail, southern little owl, desert chat, common sparrow, Spanish sparrow, white wagtail, pochard, white stork, black stork, spoonbill, Egyptian swift, little stint, Temninck's stint, wood sandpiper, Dalmatian pelican, little green bee-eater, common bee-eater and blue-cheeked bee-eater, great spotted cuckoo, sand-martin, osprey, long-legged buzzard, hooded crow, brown-backed raven, blue-throated robin, Norfolk plover (thick-knee'd bustard), peregrine and lanner falcons, merlins, rock thrush, blue rock thrush, etc. Among rare birds shot in 1889 were the *Falco Babylonicus* and the African buzzard.

CHAPTER VIII.

Luxor—Assouan.

Luxor is becoming more and more popular every winter, and as the season is a short one patients have hardly time to get tired of its monotony. A bright sunny sky, combined with healthy outdoor exercise and interesting sights to visit, is a great help towards cheerfulness, and to this we may add a dry bracing climate, and freedom from rain and all atmospheric impurities.

Dr. Patterson long ago described the Egyptian climate as possessing the warmth of Madeira, without its terrible damp and relaxing influence. The days for sending consumptive patients to hot, damp climates are almost at an end. In writing of Luxor I cannot do better than supplement Dr. Maclean's * pamphlet, which appeared after his death, and contained his own experiences as an invalid during the winters of 1877-8-9.

* "Hints for Invalids and Travellers, with Observations on the Climate of Luxor and Egypt." 1881.

Luxor is a large village of 4000 natives, is 450 miles south of Cairo, and must be reached from Cairo or Assiout by steamer or dahabiyeh.

Season.—Those who wish to make the voyage up the Nile in a dahabiyeh, and then live in it at or near Luxor, should start from Cairo at the end of November, because they will then have a delightful summer trip without cold winds. After the middle of December the north wind, which is so pleasant on land, is apt to be piercingly cold for invalids on the river, and requires the use of thick clothes and rugs. Invalids going up in a steamer from Cairo should leave not later than the third week of December, because they will thus avoid the rain and cloudiness to which Cairo is then liable. Lastly, those patients who leave Cairo later than Christmas Day should shorten the Nile trip by taking train to Assiout, or must be content to be kept well out of harm's way on the river north of that town. At Assiout they will find a fair hotel and some English officials.

Patients begin to leave Luxor at any time after the middle of February, and very few are up the river as late as the middle of April.

The English doctor is in residence at Luxor Hotel from the middle of December to the end of March, and there is now also an English chaplain. During the whole season there are, of course, constant relays of visitors, who stop for a few days on the way up and down the Nile.

Hotels.—There are two good hotels, the better of which is kept by one of Messrs. Cook's agents. It was opened at the end of 1877, and, though it has been constantly enlarged, it is always full during the season, and rooms must therefore be engaged in advance. There is accommodation for about a hundred visitors, and at the Karnak Hotel for about half that number. Until 1888 most of the Luxor Hotel rooms were built in a single line from north to south, so as to receive full benefit of morning and afternoon sun, and the rooms were on two floors, the ground floor being raised four steps above the ground. The walls are purposely built of rough bricks of great thickness, so that they can be kept cool on hot days, and will retain their heat during winter nights. But I found that invalids had to go into the open air to get from their bedroom or sitting-room to the *table d'hôte*, and the ever-willing proprietor only required to have this disadvantage pointed out to him, to construct a large dining-room, two drawing-rooms, and over these bedrooms with a central passage, which allow delicate visitors to ascend without meeting the night air. Healthy visitors find no inconvenience from occupying the older rooms. Electric bells have been set up, and earth-closets with good ventilation have been renewed. The hotel stands in a beautiful garden of sweet-smelling plants, and is distant about 350 yards from the Nile. Excellent milk and other provisions can be obtained. There are no mosquitoes or sand-flies, but often a plague of house-flies. The dogs at night have sometimes been a nuisance, but they can be destroyed by the police if proper representation is made, either locally or to Cairo.

Drinking-water is taken as usual from the Nile above the watering-place of the town, and then filtered in the ordinary way with big porous jars.

Clothing should be as for summer and autumn in the south of England. Flannel suits supplemented by a belt are very useful for both sexes by day and night. Ladies should avoid black dresses on account of the all-pervading sand, and they will require wash-leather or other gloves for donkey-riding. Sun-hats will be wanted in February and March.

Climate.—The invalid who seriously wishes to get full benefit from his stay will not be out before 10 a.m. or after sunset, and on cold days this period should be shortened. It cannot too often be repeated that the night air is very cold in comparison to that of the day, and also that whenever the temperature in Egypt is lower than 60° Fahr. it seems unpleasantly cool. But the healthy visitor may be out all day long, and the delicate one should be abroad as much as possible during the warm hours.

Luxor is on the right bank of the Nile, 292 feet above the level of the sea, in latitude 25° 40' N., and longitude 32° 35' E. Immediately opposite and lying at a lower level, is the great plain of Thebes, stretching to the Libyan hills of limestone.

Reference to Table V. shows that the corrected readings of the barometer (Fortin's) are always low and very steady till the hot weather begins. During November and December they were taken daily at 11.30 a.m.; and during the other three months, three times a day, at 9 a.m., 3 p.m., and 6 p.m.

The absolute maximum temperature for November was 94° on the 4th; for December, 77°; for January, Maclean once registered 83°; for February, 80° and 86°; and at the end of March the heat reaches even 110°, according to the same observer. The thermometers were hung in a north verandah, four feet from the ground, two feet from a wall, and protected from the wind. Of the solar temperatures in vacuo, the highest I find recorded are 164° on November 3, and 155° on March 13.

But, as I have said before, the highest and

TABLE V.

	Barometer.	Temperature.							Humidity.	Clouds, 0-10.	Ozone, 0-10.	Wind.	
		Mean of maxima.	Mean of minima.	Mean of means.	Mean maximum in sun.	Mean of daylight.	Mean of bedroom.	Mean daily range.				Direction.	Force, 0-12.
November ...	30·048	78·99	62·1	—	145·1	—	—	—	—	—	—	S.W.	·1
December ...	29·997	70	53·6	—	140·2	—	—	—	—	—	—	N.E.	1·8
January ...	29·951	65·1	41·3	56·7	130·8	61·3	64·2	23·7	53·2	2·9	4·1	N.W.	1
February ...	29·968	70·6	42·4	62·6	133	66·9	66·4	31·7	51	1·9	4·3	N.W.	1·1
March ...	29·787	80·1	47·6	66·9	147·1	77·2	77·6	38·4	45	2·1	2·9	{N.W. / N.E.}	·7

The observations for November and December were taken in 1881; those for the other months in 1878 and 1882.

lowest temperatures are not those of chief interest to the delicate visitor. He should rather consult the Table to see the average heat during the day out of doors, and the average cold of his bedroom by night. During the three months when some patients are advised to be at Luxor rather than at Cairo—December, January, February—both the daylight and bedroom temperatures are always above $60°$, and generally above $63°$ Fahr. This is the great feature of Luxor—a dry warmth during the very months when it is generally so damp and warm, or damp and cold, elsewhere. The increase in the mean daylight temperature of February over that of January is chiefly due to the increase of the daily maximum, but slightly also to the increased height of the daily minimum temperature. The remarkable uniformity of the bedroom temperature is worth noticing, and can be explained as follows. The walls, it may be remembered, are very thick, and built of crude bricks, and these, while absorbing a great deal of heat during the day, keep the extreme heat out of the room; but at night, when radiation commences, they part with their acquired surplus heat before the bedroom air can approach the temperature of the external air. By a little judicious management, opening windows to catch the sun, and shutting them again at sunset, the invalid can easily avoid all cold air, and the risks of a sudden drop of the thermometer. In March it will often be necessary to pursue the opposite tactics, and shut windows during the greatest heat of the day, to keep the bedroom from getting too hot. This was not done in March, 1878, and consequently the bedroom average jumped up to over 77°. Dr. Maclean made some further experiments, to show that the lowest temperature in the bedroom was usually 20° higher than the lowest temperature in the shade, and that a low bedroom heat depends chiefly on the presence of a low shade minimum.

The daily range of the thermometer is always very great, as one would expect in an inland dry country of the latitude of Luxor. The temperature falls at night, in consequence of the rapid radiation of heat which obtains under a cloudless sky. But the range of maximum heat from one day to another, for the first three months of the year, is 3·1°, 4·7°, 3·8°, showing that during the portion of the twenty-four hours available for the invalid the climate is remarkably equal.

The humidity is a good deal lower than that of Cairo, being 16·5 per cent. less in January, 15 less in February, and 11 less in March. The extremes in January, 1878, at Luxor, were 74 and 33; in February, 67 and 27; and in March the maximum moisture only reached 60, while the minimum fell to 21 per cent.

Rain is indeed rare at Luxor, for there was none in November and December, 1881, and this is by no means unusual. In January, 1882, there was none; but in 1878 there was one shower, and another in January 1888. In the month of February, 1878, there was a shower, another in 1882, again in 1887, and three minutes' rain was recorded by Dr. Boase in 1888.

In 1878, 1882, and 1888, no rain was noted in March. There would thus seem to be only two or three days in the year when rain falls at Luxor. Thunder and lightning are rarer still.

The amount of cloud is very little in the year, but the sky was noted as being completely overcast four times in January, once in February, and three times in March.

The amount of ozone was estimated by noting the depth of the staining produced in a piece of paper prepared with iodide of potassium and starch, after it had been exposed to the air in a double metallic gauze cage. Dr. Maclean pointed out that when the barometer stood high, and the temperature not great, the largest amounts of ozone were present, while little ozone was indicated with a low barometer on a hot day.

The wind's maximum force was 4 in January,

3 in February, and only 2 in March. The duststorms are often troublesome, though not numerous. A moderate breeze some four or five times a month carries with it a great quantity of dust, and this becomes more frequent after February.

It should be hardly necessary to say that no patients with advanced phthisis ought to be sent to winter at Luxor; neither should any of those who require to be surrounded with all modern luxuries and the treasures of culinary art. Patients with weak hearts and enlarged congested livers would be better in Cairo. Some few people who cannot, or will not, ride the ass of the country, have had themselves carried in litters to see the sights of the neighbourhood.

Amusements.— Unlimited donkey-riding and sketching are always to be had. The curio-lover may collect many authentic and a few manufactured antiquities; the sportsman can get good quail and duck-shooting with the help of a guide, and he may, if he chooses, shoot birds for a collection, jackals, and occasionally hyænas. There is not much fishing or boating, but excellent bathing, though the swimmer must be warned that the current is often swift—three miles an hour—and the banks are dangerously precipitate cliffs.

There are good postal and telegraph arrangements. There are enough local officials to provide an amusement committee, if the visitors have recourse to them.

Sight-seeing.—Close to the village of Luxor and its hotels are the two Luxor Temples, and a pleasant walk along the Avenue of Sphinxes takes us to the well-known wonders of Karnak. On the opposite side of the Nile are the Temples of Rameses I. and II., the Rameseum, the Colossi of the Eighteenth Dynasty, the Temples of Rameses III., Thothmes III., beautifully preserved sculptures, the Tombs of the Kings and other humbler folk, of the Queens, and lastly of hundreds of early Christians. All these remains, and many more of Thebes and its necropolis, contrive to make sunny Luxor a very delightful and interesting winter retreat.

A society, with its head-quarters in London, has just been started for the preservation of ancient monuments in Egypt. An estimate of the cost of the most necessary work, such as clearing away rubbish, strengthening pillars, draining off water, etc., shows that £2055 is wanted for Luxor, £3140 for Karnak, and £3400 for Thebes, Esneh, and Edfu. It is to be hoped that money will soon be forthcoming to preserve all temples from the depredation of time, thieves, and tourists.

Assouan.

There is no hotel as yet at the First Cataract, but we ought soon to see one built, for winter residents at Luxor would find it an agreeable change to go now and then to Assouan; and Shellal, opposite the island of Philæ, has been recommended as a perfect sanatorium by Dr. Abbate Pasha.

Assouan is 133 miles higher up the river than Luxor—that is, 583 miles south of Cairo. The temple of Esneh is only 35 miles from Luxor, and Edfu temple is half-way to Assouan; then, 26 miles further on, we come to the sights of Silsileh, and then the temple of Kom Ombo, a few miles north of Assouan.

Assouan has a varied native population of about 9000, and is well guarded by forts, and by 2000 Egyptian troops under English officers.

Visitors will be interested in the granite quarries, rocks of schist, granite, and basalt, Sir F. Grenfell's tombs, Elephantine Island, the shooting of the cataract, and the lovely temple on the Island of Philæ.

Temperature.—No regular meteorological records have been taken at Assouan, but the Army Medical Staff took a few notes during the Nile expedition of 1885-6, and the following Table is a *précis* of them :—

TABLE VI.

	Temperature.			Rain.	Wind.
	Mean of maxima.	Mean of minima.	Mean of means.		
December	75·7	54·6	65·1	Nil.	N.
January	74·8	51·7	63·3	Nil.	{ N.W. N.
February	78·9	55·2	67	Nil.	N.
March	84	58·6	71·3	Nil.	N.

No barometrical readings were taken. The observations were made twice daily at 9 a.m. and 3 p.m., and show a temperature record about 5° Fahr. higher than at Luxor. The air is said to be more free of dust-storms than at Luxor, and by some the winter climate is preferred.

Voyage to Second Cataract.—It is not now possible to go beyond Wady Halfa, but those who wish to see the forts there and the Temple of Abu Simbel can do so by spending three extra weeks in a dahabiyeh, or one week in a steamer. It is 210 miles from Philæ to Wady Halfa.

Defences of Egypt.—Many visitors, chiefly Americans, were deterred from coming to Egypt in the **winter of 1888-9**, because of the Soudanese raids outside the town of Suakin. It may therefore be wise to state exactly what is the disposition of the troops which have to defend Egypt and its visitors from any hypothetical hordes of invading dervishes. Suakin is a port on the Red Sea, which by a fast-sailing steamer can only be reached in eight days from Cairo. It is well fortified and garrisoned by 3000 Egyptian and black soldiers, officered by the British army, who are well able to repel any advances of the Soudanese, and can, if necessary, be strengthened by English troops.

At Wady Halfa, which is eight hundred miles from Cairo, and separated from it by a distance which can only be traversed in ten days by the fastest steamers, there are more than 3000 Egyptian and black soldiers, again commanded by Englishmen. There are also many strong forts, for the English policy is to act entirely on the defensive until the raids of the Soudanese become so impudent that it is absolutely necessary to chastise them, as in August, 1889. At Assouan, I have already said, there are forts manned by 2000 of the Egyptian army. In Cairo and Alexandria there are 3000 English soldiers of all branches of the service, who can be moved to any spot should danger threaten, and can be reinforced from Malta, Gibraltar, Cyprus, or from troops passing through the Suez Canal to or from India. The Soudanese are likely to remain unsettled, but I hope I have said enough to show that they will not be allowed to do more than occasionally harass the frontier stations of Egypt.

In conclusion, I have only to add that the Egyptian police is recruited from the army, and it again is officered by the English, and ample provision exists for preventing any internal disturbance among one of the most peaceful and least criminal populations of the world.

CHAPTER IX.

ALEXANDRIA—RAMLEH.

ALEXANDRIA once possessed a great reputation for salubrity, and was much recommended by the ancient physicians for diseases of the chest. But the modern city is no favourite with invalids, and tourists, obliged to use it as a port of entry, hurry on to Cairo because they can find nothing of sight-seeing to detain them. During the early months of the year Alexandria is subject to rain, gales, and cold, but in April the weather is often pleasanter than in Cairo, and it is at this time that invalids for whom Europe is not yet warm enough are recommended to stay, not in Alexandria itself, but in the suburb of Ramleh near by. They will find refreshing sea-breezes, instead of the liability to khamseen wind in Cairo, a temperature which is not too high, and a degree of humidity which is not excessive. The days are bright and sunny, and the nights not too cold. In the town of Alexandria there are two first-class hotels, several smaller ones, three or four "pensions," and a dozen lodging-houses, two clubs, three theatres, and streets of European shops. Very little trace of the bombardment and fire of 1882 remains, and since £4,000,000 of indemnity were paid by the Egyptian Government, building has been stimulated to such an extent that there are many new houses and shops which cannot find a tenant.

Among medical men there is a well-known Scotchman, who with his assistants has for three decades administered to the wants of the British colony, and he has as colleagues a dozen Europeans of the first rank, besides an American dentist and two oculists. There are three druggists commanding confidence, three trained English nurses for private cases at their own homes, and three excellent European hospitals where private patients are received.

The *water-supply* of the town is excellent, and is in the hands of an English company, which has a monopoly for ever, and is represented on the spot by an energetic and highly intelligent English civil engineer. The water is obtained from the Mahmoudieh canal, which branches off the Nile at Atfeh; but if, during low Nile, there is any danger of the river at Atfeh becoming brackish, the supply is taken from higher up the Nile near Cairo. The banks of the canal are inspected by watchmen, to prevent natives from throwing carcasses or emptying drains into it, and they also flush the canal every ten days with 500,000 tons of Nile water.

At high Nile the water is so muddy that it is necessary to mix with it alum and iron before it is pumped into the filter-beds. Also if chemical analysis shows an abnormal percentage of organic matter, permanganate of soda is mixed with the water before it reaches the filter-beds. There are three filter-beds, each 2400 yards square, and covered with wood. The beds are 2 ft. 6 in. deep, and consist of sand, which is brought from the sea-shore near Damietta, and of four different sizes of gravel, laid on bricks, and so placed as to make a ready communication between the lower layers and the pumps for cleansing purposes. The sand is well washed in water, and the beds cleaned every nine days. From the filter-beds the water is pumped into a reservoir, and thence into Alexandria, at the rate of 26,000 cubic metres a day.

Though the water-supply is so well cared for, the *drainage* of Alexandria cannot be commended. Since 1871 the streets of the town have been paved, like Naples, with slabs of lava from Catania, and the drains, originally laid down by the Paving Commission for storm-water, have been used as overflows for the cesspools under the houses. The culverts run out to the sea-shore, but some are built with an insufficient fall, and others ventilate untrapped into the streets, accounting for many of the unpleasant odours of the town. The cesspools not running into these culverts are emptied by carts on the sea-shore near the town.

Ramleh.

Ramleh has a station of its own (Sidi Gabir) upon the line from Cairo to Alexandria, but if carriages are required to meet the traveller there they must be previously ordered from Alexandria. With the exception of a few private carriages, life at Ramleh is carried on on donkey-back. During the daytime trains run every hour or half-hour from Alexandria to the seven stations, which are only about half a mile apart. Each house stands proudly in its own grounds, and varies in character from a limestone shanty to a pretentious two-storied *châlet*. The prevailing wind blows refreshingly from the sea; there are miles of desert to explore on the land side, pretty gardens to the straggling houses, and, besides representatives of Greece and many other nations, a colony of English officials and merchants who are famous for their hospitality and their lawn-tennis parties. Ramleh now has a scattered population of about four thousand, but has only been inhabited for the last thirty years; and crouching next to the garden-walls of merchant princes are still to be seen patched Bedouin tents, whose mysterious inmates are a relic of the Arabs who levied blackmail on the first English settlers, and professed to keep the rest of their tribesmen at a distance.

For *hotels*, there are thirty-two bedrooms at San Stefano, a highly commended Beau Sejour, and two smaller hotels, besides an English private boarding-house. San Stefano also embraces clubrooms, excellent swimming-baths for both sexes, electric-lighting, a European string-band, weekly afternoon dances for children, evening parties for adults, etc. The height of the season is from June 15 to October 15, but the hotel is open earlier in the year.

Some Greek doctors are resident in Ramleh, and there is now a chemist; but most residents prefer to get their medical help direct from Alexandria. There is a Greek *church* and an Italian Catholic; while in Alexandria there are Church of England, Church of Scotland, German and French Protestant, Roman Catholic, and many other places of worship.

The *conservancy* arrangements are of too primitive a character. Many English houses are provided with earth-closets; the rest have cesspools draining away into the porous sand. Up till now

Ramleh has been a wonderfully healthy spot; but the day will come when the subsoil will be saturated with all the water used for the gardens, baths, and kitchens, and some scheme of drainage will be necessary.

The *water-supply* is pumped straight from the canal of the Alexandria Company, unfiltered, to a reservoir, and thence to Ramleh at the rate of 12,000 cubic metres a day. For use in the house, it is then filtered through native porous jars. The greater part of the water is of course used for the private gardens, where, besides many English flowers and fruits, one sees oleanders, point-settias, hibiscus, bougainvillia, begonia trees, indiarubber trees towering almost as high as the palms, and grapes, bananas, oranges, figs, and melons. The desert abounds in a great variety of small flowers; and one of the features of this neighbourhood is the ice-plant (*Mesembryanthemum cristallinum*). Altogether the botanist will find more than two hundred specimens of interest in and near Ramleh, while the sea-coast is covered with beautiful shells.

Amusements.—The English residents boast of as many as fifteen lawn-tennis courts, a book-club, and even a race meeting during two days in June. There are paper chases on ponies and donkeys, and an occasional gymkhana, or cricket-match, when the English regiment quartered in Alexandria vies with the naval and civilian population. Needless to say, there are many hospitable evening parties, and, as the weather gets warmer, moonlight donkey-excursions for the adventurous. Bathing and fishing are always within reach; and the Alexandria harbour provides excellent sailing. From November to March, plenty of duck and snipe shooting can be had at Damietta, and within an hour of Ramleh; and for about a month from the middle of March, there is good quail-shooting at Abu Homos, Damanhour, etc. From July to October, foreign sportsmen shoot doves, hoopoes, and other birds in the neighbourhood; and in September the quail come again in such numbers that one day (in 1887) two hundred and forty were shot by a Greek resident.

Sight-seeing.—Alas! it is only with the eye of faith that we can see relics of the famous city founded 2200 years ago, and once boasting a muster-roll of 500,000 souls. An English sentry paces above the ruins of the Museum where Euclid, Aristophanes, and Hypatia were once professors. Where the Grand Square now stands was a long row of obelisks and sphinxes leading to the famous Library; but of old buildings nothing now remains but a granite pillar or two in the native quarter of the town. The two obelisks brought by a Cæsar from Heliopolis did indeed mark the site of the Temple where honours were paid to dead and living Cæsars, and where to-day the British consul has his modern house; but, as every one knows, they were carried away to lose their hieroglyphics in the ungenial climates of London and New York. The very tomb of the great Alexander is lost to us, and has almost inspired Dr. Schliemann to a search-expedition for the mausoleum of the Ptolemies. Pompey's Pillar, as it is erroneously called, is only interesting to us because it is the sole relic of the city where Antony wooed Cleopatra, and of the time when Alexandria was the commercial centre of the world, and Egypt was the principal granary of Rome.

There are now only about fifteen cisterns in the town, though in 1869 there were ten times that number to be seen. This is only an illustration of the destruction which has visited the city under Arab, Turkish, and Egyptian rulers. These cisterns are large, built under the houses, arched, and coated with plaster.

Next in interest are the Catacombs, or remains of the ancient Necropolis, once upon a time surrounded by vineyards and gardens. They are cut in the calcareous rock facing the sea, between Gabarri and Mex, and an early Christian church, best visited by boat, is hewn out of the rock at

Ooma-ka-bebi. Antiquarians may be interested, too, in a fortified Greek church, to which the English residents used to be escorted by a Janissary for Protestant services so late as 1840, before the English church was built. Fort Pharos, on the site of one of the seven wonders of the world, and other forts still show traces of their bombardment in 1882. Visitors are taken to see the Khedive's yacht *Mahroussa*, his palace at Ras-el-Teen, the view from the lighthouse, and from the signal-station on Fort Napoleon, and to the drive and gardens on the Mahmoudieh Canal, where an Egyptian band plays twice a week. In Ramleh itself there are the " spouting rocks," where the sea rushes through some openings which have been artificially enlarged, and near by are palm groves and curious sand-heaps (? tumuli). In 1889, a Roman tomb with coloured stucco interior was discovered, close to some catacombs on the sea-shore. These tombs are of pagan officers, probably from Cæsar's camp, which was standing twenty years ago, and demolished to build a palace, now in its turn abandoned. Here was Nicopolis, where Augustus defeated Antony, and where Sir Ralph Abercromby died while beating the French under General Menou in 1801.

The only expeditions in the neighbourhood are to Rosetta, which is now almost deserted, and to

Alexandria—Ramleh.

Aboukir, where the lake is now being drained, and there are forts connected by torpedoes with the bay in which Nelson fought the Battle of the Nile, and his opponent's "boy stood on the burning deck, whence all but he had fled." Near Aboukir are the remains of Canopus, with granite columns lying about, and whence, in 1888, the statue of Rameses II. was transferred to the Boulak Museum.

Table VII. has been compiled from statistics kindly furnished me by M. A. Pirona, of Alexandria, and is based upon his meteorological observations of the nineteen years, 1870–88, for the Central Meteorological Institute of Vienna. His instruments were made in Vienna, and rectified at the Royal Observatory there. The readings of the barometer are at freezing-point, sixty-two feet above sea-level, and were taken at 9 a.m., 3 p.m., and 9 p.m. The mean temperatures are based on records at 9 a.m., 9 p.m., maxima and minima, and coincide with some observations made in 1847–49. It will be noticed that the prevailing wind is always straight from the Mediterranean. The number of rainy days in March is 4·5; in the month of April, only 1·5; and in May the average further falls to 0·7.

These are the three months when Ramleh is at its best, and can be safely recommended to those on their way from Cairo to Europe.

TABLE VII.

	Barometer.	Thermometer Fahr.			Humidity.	Rain in inches.	Clouds. 0–10.	Ozone. 0–14.	Wind.	
		Mean of maxima.	Mean of Minima.	Mean of Means.	Relative.				Direction.	Force. 0–10.
January ...	30·01	64	53·2	58·1	67	2·33	4	7·4	N.	2·5
February ...	30·01	64·2	54	58·6	65	1·43	4	7·8	N.W.	2·5
March ...	29·94	68	56	61·6	65	·78	3	8·1	N.W.	2·7
April ...	29·90	73	60·6	66	66	·12	2	7·9	N.	2·5
May ...	29·91	75·4	65·6	70	70	·03	2	7·8	N.	2·2
June ...	29·86	79·6	71·2	75	72	—	1	7·5	N.	2·3
July ...	29·78	81·2	74·8	77·6	75	—	1	7·6	N.N.W.	2·4
August ...	29·79	82·4	76·1	79	73	·11	1	7·5	N.	2
September ...	29·89	81·2	74·3	77·4	69	·33	2	7·2	N.	2·3
October ...	29·96	79·2	70·6	74·6	68	1·32	2	6·7	N.	2·1
November ...	30	73·4	64	68·2	67	1·32	3	7	N.	2·2
December...	30·02	67·8	57	62	67	1·79	4	6·9	N.	2·4
Average ...	29·925	74·1	64·8	69	68·6	8·24	2·4	7·4	N.	2·3

APPENDIX.

IN the introductory chapter I have already mentioned in a general way the diseases which are likely to be benefited by wintering in Egypt, and now I propose to consider the question a little more in detail, referring only to the most common diseases which I have met with amongst health-seekers in Cairo.

Phthisis.—Commencing with pulmonary consumption, it may be stated that cases of acute tuberculosis or acute phthisis are not sent to Egypt as a rule, because of their rapid fatality and because the state of the patient is so serious as to prevent the desirability of transport. The few patients I have seen with scrofulous phthisis associated with caries of vertebræ, psoas abscess, or fistula *in ano*, have generally done very well in Cairo, but some of them have died within a few months after leaving for Europe.

Perhaps I may be allowed here to quote the statistics of the influence of foreign climates in consumption published by Dr. C. T. Williams: 251 cases were sent to various places in the Riviera, south of Europe, north of Africa, and Atlantic islands. Twenty patients spent twenty-six winters in Egypt, and furnished "by far the finest land result" of the experiment; 65 per cent. improved, 25 per cent. remained stationary, and only 10 per cent. became worse. It is a matter for congratulation that the expense of the trip to Cairo and the ascent of the Nile is now so much reduced that the country is thrown open to large numbers of patients who have hitherto been prevented from coming. Out of 45 cases that I have seen with unmistakable phthisis, 69 per cent. improved, 20 per cent. remained stationary, and only 11 per cent. grew worse (including three deaths in Egypt).

My figures are, therefore, confirmatory of the results previously obtained by Dr. Williams. The three deaths which occurred in Egypt were cases in the last stage of phthisis, which died soon after arrival, and of course ought not to have been sent abroad. I can only repeat—what every one knows already—that threatened cases of phthisis, with or without a bad family history, can apparently be prevented from developing in a pure, dry, warm climate; that incipient cases can be improved and perhaps cured; that chronic cases can remain stationary, so that their lives are definitely prolonged; but that advanced cases with disease in both lungs and a temperature every night above the normal cannot be cured by a change of climate, though their disease may, under fortunate circumstances, be arrested, and their days consequently may be enlivened and prolonged.

Perhaps the most satisfactory case to send abroad is the overgrown boy or girl with winter cough, insufficient expansion of chest, and general lassitude. Such patients require little or no medical treatment, gain weight and breadth of body and mind, and return to their work at home with healthy vigour. Next, if any cases of phthisis are to be sent abroad, they must be either those which, though anatomically advanced, are chronic or quiescent, or those in the earliest possible stage.

Now, in the case of these latter, the patients and their friends are least likely to think of the scheme, or even to suspect the disease. It therefore rests with the medical attendant, where he thinks fit, to order for his patient a continuance for some months of an equable warm climate, such as is provided by a summer in England, a winter in Egypt, and a second summer in England. When a patient

Appendix. 147

in whom phthisis is suspected goes or is taken by his relatives to a doctor to have his chest examined, it may generally be prophesied either that there is no ground for uneasiness, or that the disease has already made distinct progress. Incipient cases which gain weight and improve in other respects during a winter abroad, often need to be reminded that the measure should be repeated a second time.

Popular young patients must often be banished from Cairo during December and January, to desert life at the Pyramids, or at Luxor, to protect them from themselves and their acquaintance, and the snares of evening engagements.

Chronic cases of undoubted phthisis do very well in Egypt, for they improve in general health, digestion, and appetite, and can often take cod-liver oil, which was previously impossible. They are encouraged by finding that they gain a little weight, and become rid of troublesome cough and expectoration. This last symptom is an important one in Egypt, and one of the first signs of the patient's improvement.

An ordinary phthisical individual complains, when he first reaches Cairo, of cough and expectoration, and the stethoscope reveals a multitude of large and small moist sounds. When he is seen again a fortnight later, these sounds have partly disappeared, he still coughs, but is surprised and sometimes alarmed to notice that the expectoration has suddenly diminished. After another week or two, he reports that he only expectorates the first thing in the morning; he seldom coughs during the day, and the stethoscope again confirms the drying-up process which is going on in the lung, which seems to be the direct result of dry air inhaled. This is not so wonderful when we remember that the average winter humidity of the Cairo air is under sixty-six per cent. (Table I.), while that of London is above ninety per cent. It would be interesting to know whether the very dry air is inimical to the life and development of the tubercle bacillus. Two cases in which bacilli were seen in London and on arrival in Cairo, and could not be found before leaving Cairo and upon returning to London, are possibly confirmatory of this suspicion.

Advanced cases of phthisis will often be much happier leading an indoor life in their own unsuitable climate than an occasional outdoor life in a more favourable one. This is especially the case if the patient has very limited means. He gains sunlight and sunheat during the day, and runs a chance of his disease being arrested; but against this he must balance draughts and irksome travelling, a paucity of fireplaces, food and habits to which he is unsuited, and exile from his home-comforts and best friends.

I have previously referred to the question as to whether it is advisable or not to send cases of hæmorrhagic phthisis to Cairo. I have not yet seen any ill result from doing so, and though I do not wish here to quote medical cases, I will give the results of the only two patients I have met, with alarming history of recent hæmoptysis. The first case, a friend, but not a patient of mine, aged 27, had copious hæmoptysis, recurring several times, followed by cough, purulent sputa, dyspnœa, and loss of weight (17½ lbs.). He was sent to Pau, Nice, Mont Dore, and eventually to Egypt. He was so weak that he had to be carried ashore at Suez, and he could not walk for more than ten minutes at a time. After six weeks in Cairo, he went to Luxor for two months in January, 1888. In March his cough and expectoration had quite ceased, and he could be out shooting for three hours at a time. He gained 19½ lbs. weight while in Egypt, and spent the following winter at Cairo and Luxor, without cough, expectoration, or hæmoptysis, but still with old physical signs at the right apex.

The second case was that of a lady, aged 19, whose father, brother, and sister, had all died of rapid phthisis with hæmoptysis. She herself had had hæmoptysis for a year, with loss of flesh, night sweats, slight cough, and signs of incipient disease at one apex. After fifteen weeks at Cairo, she had gained 15 lbs. weight, and there was general improvement in every respect, except that she occasionally had blood-stained expectoration in the morning. In September, 1889, her doctor reported that her improvement continued, both lungs were sound, and there had been no more hæmorrhage.

There is, as might be expected, great improvement in the cases of lung-disease which apparently begin as pleurisy, pleuro-pneumonia, or pneumonia, and anæmic, delicate-looking people go home sunburnt, and able to walk, ride, and play lawn-tennis, after two or three months' stay in Cairo. The cases which do not improve much are often those who will not stay indoors after twilight, and expose themselves to cold and damp during December and January.

I have seen considerable improvement in some cases of laryngeal phthisis, but more in the general state than locally. Most of the cases of advanced phthisis which have grown worse in Egypt have been complicated with chronic diarrhœa. There are several apparently healthy residents now in Cairo who originally came there from Europe for their health, some of them having had hæmoptysis and other lung symptoms.

Chronic bronchitis.—A good many emphysematous patients come to Cairo every winter, because they find they can get through the cold months with less cough, less discomfort, and far less confinement. Those whose bronchial tubes are irritated by the fine dust in the air on sand-storm days must then remain shut up in their houses, just as they would to avoid fog, rain, and east wind elsewhere.

Asthma.—All the cases that I have seen in Egypt have improved and done well, excepting two. Several former asthmatic patients have settled down as residents in the country, and one English lady, who has had dry asthma for twenty years, comes every year to Cairo and the Nile because she is quite well there. Her brother and other relations suffer from asthma, and she herself can live happily in London, but in no other part of England that she has yet discovered. She gets slight asthma in Alexandria, and is relieved directly she reaches Cairo.

Of the two cases in which there was no improvement, one was an English officer who suffered at all times and in all places except when he was on the sea. At Suakin and Alexandria he was comfortable, but in Cairo he was liable to be laid up once a fortnight, and then had to go a short yachting cruise to get quite rid of his asthma. The second case was a very inveterate one, for the lady had been troubled with asthma and occasional bronchitis for more than twenty years. At Cairo and Luxor she still had asthma every morning, but in a modified degree. She believed that she obtained no good from a dry climate, and like the officer, she pined for the sea air, and stated that in England, Brighton was the place where she had least asthma.

It is not difficult to understand that asthmatic patients who have immunity from their attacks in damp sea air, may obtain no relief from dry desert air, and the converse is also apparently true.

To secure the maximum benefit from the climate of Egypt it seems to be necessary for asthmatic people to keep in the same temperature as much as possible, and therefore to avoid night air. One patient, who had had chronic bronchitis and asthma for two years, obtained great good from six months spent in Egypt, and though in the succeeding year and a half she has had pleurisy, she has had no more bronchitis or asthma.

Rheumatism in an acute form is practically unknown among the natives and Europeans in Egypt, but I have seen two cases among young English patients. One caught cold at Suez, and had in Cairo her second attack of rheumatic fever; the other patient had also had a previous attack, and consequent heart-disease, and caught a chill in Cairo during the winter. The climate is excellent for all forms of chronic rheumatism, and for patients convalescing from acute rheumatism contracted elsewhere. Rheumatic pains and aches are seldom met with except when Cairo is less dry than usual. The sulphur baths at Helouan are, of course, a useful help to the dry climate.

Rheumatoid arthritis I have only once seen in an Egyptian; but every winter there are numbers of Europeans who come to Cairo to get rid of their pain, stiffness, and swelling, and to try and postpone their next acute attack. All those that I have met with have greatly improved, and among them is the case of a lady who for this disease had had a previous experience of Buxton, Bath, San Remo, Cannes, Algiers, Pau, Biarritz, Wiesbaden, and Spain. She has now been for three years running to Cairo, and believes that the climate is the best she has yet tried. She has had rheumatic attacks for fifteen years, and for nearly all that time has had her joints anchylosed and swollen, so that the only ones which remained free were the hips, toes, and vertebræ.

At the end of the second winter in Cairo, she could stand and walk alone and almost upright, and was delighted with her own activity. She took no drugs, had no sulphur baths, and no massage during that winter, and only consulted her doctor upon one day.

She has a distinct family predisposition towards rheumatism; her father was very gouty, mother rheumatic, mother's father very gouty, and all maternal relatives are rheumatic. She has lost a sister of rheumatic fever, and has living a brother who has heart-disease and has had rheumatic fever three times, and a sister who has chronic rheumatism after an acute attack.

Another case was that of a lady with a strong family history of rheumatism, and a personal history of four years. She had previously tried Buxton, Strathpeffer, Wildbad, sulphur baths, and massage, with a little temporary improvement after each. When she reached Cairo she could walk stiffly, but for three years had been unable to run, dance, play lawn-tennis, or walk downstairs. Two months later she could run a few steps, walk downstairs quickly and without ungainly gait, and she had very little pain, and much less cracking in the knee-joints. The improvement was chiefly due to sunshine and the dry climate, and when the air of Cairo became hot and dry in April she improved all the more. The following August she could play golf in Scotland for two hours at a time, and had had no return of stiffness in the joints, though the previous summer she had been unable to walk on the links even with the aid of a stick. These brief notes of two cases are sufficient to show that Egypt is worth a trial to sufferers from rheumatoid arthritis.

I have seen great improvement and eventual cure in some severe cases of G. rheumatism, the hot dry climate being the only relieving agent. One patient arrived wholly unable to walk, with one lower extremity completely stiff, after severe arthritis keeping him fourteen weeks in bed. In two months and a half he could walk up and downstairs, but could not yet kneel; later on he almost recovered in England.

Gout, again, is an unknown disease among the people of Egypt, and all chronic cases are liable to be improved there, and the chances of an acute attack are lessened.

Heart disease and kidney disease patients are often sent to Egypt, the former, because it is a country where active exercise is not required, and the individual can keep himself warm without any trouble; the latter, because the skin will relieve the kidneys of much otherwise necessary work.

Anæmia, with the train of symptoms with which all doctors are so familiar in young girls, is the prominent sign of a disorder which is tolerably certain to improve in Cairo. There is a healthy outdoor life, with plenty of light and warmth, and a sufficiency of daily interest. The patient soon becomes able to eat and digest, and to take preparations of iron which had hitherto seemed impossible. This has been a result quickly arrived at in most cases.

Hepatic diseases.—As the climate of Cairo in winter is

not very unlike that of England during a dry summer, I see no reason why patients with liver disease should not be sent there or up the Nile, though perhaps it would be unwise to let them remain after February at Luxor. The ordinary individual with cirrhosis or other result of alcoholic tendency, improves temporarily while in Egypt, because he finds it easier to do without stimulants. The peaceful life on a dahabiyeh with agreeable company is sometimes very useful in such cases.

Lastly, that great and increasing multitude of interesting patients, the neurotic, men and women, are without exception so content in Egypt that they have but little time or inclination to consider their complaints.

THE END.

www.ingramcontent.com/pod-product-compliance
Lightning Source LLC
Chambersburg PA
CBHW030255170426
43202CB00009B/756